AN INTRODUCTION TO
FILM ANALYSIS

AN INTRODUCTION TO

FILM ANALYSIS

Technique and Meaning in Narrative Film

Michael Ryan and Melissa Lenos

continuum

NEW YORK • LONDON

2012

The Continuum International Publishing Group Inc
80 Maiden Lane, New York, NY 10038

The Continuum International Publishing Group Ltd
The Tower Building, 11 York Road, London SE1 7NX

www.continuumbooks.com

Library of Congress Cataloging-in-Publication Data
A catalog record for this book is available from the Library of Congress.

ISBN: HB: 978-0-8264-3001-4
       PB: 978-0-8264-3002-1

Typeset by Fakenham Prepress Solutions, Fakenham, Norfolk NR21 8NN
Printed in the United States of America

For Gabriel

Contents

43-50
1 56-168
109-131

Acknowledgements

We are grateful to the following people for their help in putting this book together:

Dudley Andrew, Warren Bass, Matthew Bernstein, Thomas Byers, Chris Cagle, Noel Carroll, Christine Erb, Lalitha Gopalan, Claudia Harken, Barbara Klinger, Akira Mazuta Lippitt, Bill Nichols, Andrew Parker, Mark David Rosenthal, Janet Staiger, and Clyde Taylor.

Frank Fulchiero and Beth Hansen provided invaluable technical and archival assistance.

Introduction

MEANING IN MOVIES

A movie is a marriage of technique and meaning. Whenever filmmakers lay out a set, direct actors to act in a certain way, place the camera in particular positions, and assemble the resulting mass of shots into a coherent narrative, they not only tell a story, they also make meaning.

FIGURE I *A Clockwork Orange*. By placing the source light behind the young men, Stanley Kubrick paints their heads black. The technique reinforces the idea that the boys lack humanity as they set about beating a helpless drunk.

Some meaning is consciously intended. For example, in *Pulp Fiction* (1994), Quentin Tarantino tells the story of a gangster who seeks redemption, and he inserts references to religious ideas in the movie, especially to the idea of making amends for the wrongs one has done. A restaurant is called the "Hawthorne Grill," a reference to the American writer Nathaniel Hawthorne who explored the issue of personal moral responsibility in his novel, *The Scarlet Letter* (1850); and a motorcycle is called "Grace," a reference to the Christian idea of divine forgiveness, which is a theme of Hawthorne's novel. These references reinforce the idea that it is possible to make amends for past wrongs and to change one's life.

Some intended meanings are not as obvious. In *The Shining* (1980), for example, Stanley Kubrick dresses a female character in red and has her walk through a hedge maze that resembles a forest in which one could easily get lost. Kubrick lets you know he is evoking the story of Little Red Riding Hood by

FIGURES II & III *Pulp Fiction*. In this film about gangsters with morals, references are made to classic American literature and familiar themes in American Protestant religion.

cutting from an image of the woman, wearing a red hooded coat and outside in nature, to an image of her husband looking like a wolf. He is about to go mad and try to murder her. Kubrick's point is that we are all animals; some of us would, under enough pressure, lapse into an animal state if civil restraints were removed.

Not all meaning in a movie is as deliberate or intentional as Tarantino's religious references or Kubrick's fairy-tale allusions. Some meanings come from the culture a filmmaker inhabits, and they enter a film without the filmmaker realizing it. We all live in cultures that shape how we think and what we believe,

FIGURES IV & V *The Shining*. The movie evokes the Red Riding Hood story, and fittingly, Jack, the murderous father, is made to look like a wolf.

and those influences often determine what kinds of movies we make. Someone who grows up in a racist culture will in all likelihood make racist movies, even though s/he may not consciously intend to do so. S/he will simply take that way of looking at things for granted. It is how s/he sees (and depicts) the world. Our cultures speak through us in ways we do not always control, and we often act, as a result, in ways that are unconscious.

For example, Alfred Hitchcock did not consciously set out in *The Birds* (1963) to make a movie that punishes independent women and urges them towards a more traditional, passive and dependent model of female identity. All of his comments about the movie suggest that he believed he was making a simple horror story. But he grew up in a conservative Catholic culture that frowned on sexually independent women, and one meaning the film conveys is that such women pose a danger to civilization. A very traditionalist conservative in regard to gender and much else, Hitchcock put his values and assumptions into the movie without being aware that he was doing so. He simply took for granted that he was making a movie about the way things are and should be. And one thing he took for granted about human life was that men should rule.

FIGURE VI *The Birds*. In order to argue that independent women should adopt more traditional gender roles, Hitchcock portrays women creating crises by assuming traditionally male roles.

Other meanings are shaped by thematic or aesthetic necessity and seem neither entirely unconscious nor entirely deliberate. Filmmakers often do things because they seem right, given the nature of the materials they are working with. The way an image is constructed might make sense in regard to a film's story or in regard to the aesthetic principles at work in the film. As a result, the image will seem to arise from the very nature of the material or from the way the story demands to be depicted. Consider an image from *The Lord of the Rings* (2001). Aragorn, the future king, stands before the broken sword of his ancestors, and behind him on the wall is a painting of one of his royal ancestor doing battle with Sauron, the evil overlord who threatens Aragorn's world. Notice how the color of Aragorn's clothing is the same as the color of the painting. His affinity with his ancestor is emphasized by the match of colors. At this point in the film, Aragorn has doubts about his ability to be king. But the image suggests that there is continuity—a royal line of descent—between him and his predecessors. The filmmakers may have made a conscious decision to make a point about Aragorn's continuity with his ancestors by matching the green color of his clothing to that of the painting behind him, but they may also simply have recognized unconsciously that the match made sense aesthetically and thematically. Either way, it has the effect it has.

FIGURE VII *The Lord of the Rings.* Color signals an affinity between a would-be king and his royal antecedents.

Not everything in a movie has a meaning in this way, however. In *Amelie* (2001), the filmmakers use red and green colors throughout. The movie is a painting, and the two major color themes match up pretty clearly with ideas about human life in the movie. But the filmmakers decided to vary the images by inserting occasional dollops of blue. No meaning is intended; it just makes for a nice visual effect because blue balances well with red and green as one of the three additive colors in cinematography.

Unintended meanings also arise from the fact that movies are connected to the social world in which they are made. *Avatar* (2009) is about the conflict between a mining company and a native tribe, but it is also about the culture war in America between liberals and conservatives regarding environmental protection, even though that culture war is not an explicit discussion point in the movie. That background debate is one of the film's meanings, one thing that influences what it is about.

FIGURE VIII *Amelie*. In this film, red is a dominant thematic color, and the filmmakers occasionally put in some blue to vary the palette.

All movies contain meanings of this sort that are historical, political, cultural, psychological, social, and economic. Movies refer to the world in which they are made in a variety of ways.

Knocked Up (2007), for example, is a romantic comedy about an unsuccessful slacker who gets a successful professional woman pregnant. She can't believe her bad luck, he his good luck. They learn to love each other in the end and make compromises regarding the tension between their respective economic prospects. The film also endorses a particular model of self-identity, economic striving, and personal success. He, in order to "win" her, must leave his all-male group of less-than-successful, druggie buddies, get a job, and set himself up in life alone in his own apartment. He must become a striving individual and assume a more responsible identity. One meaning of the movie then might be that, to have a beautiful, successful wife and a family in this day and age, you must work hard, be responsible, and leave the immature, self-indulgent habits of childhood behind. The intended meaning of the movie would seem to be "to have a wife, you need to get a life."

But the movie also refers to the world in which it was made. Since the 1970s, because it chose to pursue conservative economic policies, the United States has transformed itself into a plutocratic society in which a minority has grown extremely wealthy while a majority gets by on much less. Survival now increasingly requires that both husband and wife work. Prior to the 1970s, it was possible for just the husband to work in order for the family to enjoy a middle-class lifestyle. But with the distribution of wealth upwards since 1980 (through deregulation of business and banking, reduced taxes on the wealthy, "free trade" policies that exported jobs overseas, and the destruction of labor unions), that social model in which male identity hinged on being the "breadwinner" has disappeared. In addition, the Feminist Movement since the 1960s opened up more career possibilities for women that were closed off to them during an earlier, more conservative era. Women with jobs are now competitors with men;

FIGURE IX *Knocked Up.* A young professional woman is dismayed to learn she is pregnant.

they have become their own breadwinners. As the old way of mating changed under pressure from the economic environment and from social movements like Feminism, men have had to come up with new criteria for status and new models of self-identity.

Knocked Up alludes to this crisis and addresses it with hope, much as a dream allows us to use our imagination to cure pain or relieve distress by turning stressful events in our daytime lives into nighttime images of success. But the distress in men's lives is real, nevertheless. And the film, even as it offers a fantasy resolution that allows a less successful man to have a successful woman, points it out to us. The story of the film is made possible by a painful reality that is in many ways at odds with the image of happy success the film offers. In addition to the intended idea it embodies about how to succeed romantically in this day and age, the film embodies this other, more problematic meaning as well.

Meaning comes in two basic forms, then. One kind of meaning is consciously intended. *Michael Clayton* (2007) is about a man who must choose between being a loyal "janitor" for his corrupt law firm, and exposing the wrongdoing of an agribusiness corporation that covers up evidence proving one of its products kills people. The film is about what it means to have moral courage. Early in the film, the filmmakers use images that portray Michael visually as someone who faces a choice between being an anonymous functionary who is as lacking in human texture as the buildings around him, and being someone who places the ethical care for others before corporate profits. The meaning of these images seems fairly clear: Michael makes himself small in a moral sense by going along with the corruption around him. The filmmakers deliberately depict the main character using images suggesting anonymity and conformity.

FIGURE X *Michael Clayton*. Michael is depicted early in the film as an anonymous functionary who does his job without thinking about how unethical it is.

Another kind of meaning is not consciously intended and comes instead from the world around a movie. It seeps into a movie without the filmmakers consciously intending to put it there. Without intending to do so, the makers of *Knocked Up* gave us a film about income inequality and about how the emergence of successful professional women in recent decades affects the lives of men. They wanted to make a funny comedy, but they also made a film about the world we live in. An awake, connected movie like *Knocked Up* that wishes to represent that world as it is must represent it as it is. In a sense, no matter how hard we dream in movies, there's no avoiding reality—because even our dreams are real.

In this book, we will be concerned with both kinds of meaning. The first part of the book deals with intended meaning, the second with a variety of meanings that are shaped by such contextual dimensions of film as economics, politics, history, and gender relations.

Let's start with intended meaning. The procedures, devices, and techniques of filmmaking both construct stories and make meaning. By asking "Why?" of any image or of any single use of a cinematic device, procedure, or technique, one begins to unfold the dimensions or levels of meaning implied by it. Why begin *The Searchers* (1956), a classic western of the 1950s, for example, with a dark image from within a house that then becomes light as a door is opened and the camera follows a female character onto a porch to gaze out onto an unaccommodating-looking landscape? Why not begin simply with a shot of the landscape? Why alternate high and low angle shots as a lawyer and a "playgirl" discuss her behavior, in *The Birds*? Why not use a two shot that fits them both into the frame? Why use blue and red colors so pervasively in *The Shining*? Why not use a more varied palette? Why move to a high overhead shot when a black lawyer finally agrees to help a victim of AIDS who has been unjustly fired, in *Philadelphia* (1993)? Why move away from single framing of each character to such an anonymous shot? Why conclude *The Talented Mr. Ripley* (1999), a film about amoral ambition, with a side shot from inside a closet whose door swings open and shut? What does the swinging closet door add that a frontal shot of his face might miss? Why in *2046* (2004) place a young prostitute in a widescreen frame that is dominated by the color green? How does this way of constructing the image depict her emotional state?

FIGURE XI *2046*. In this painterly film, images are constructed to depict changes in the emotional economy between a man and a prostitute who falls in love with him.

Filmmakers use technique to make meaning. Film analysis studies those techniques in order to determine what those meanings are.

Each technique such as the close-up, the long take, and low-key lighting can be used to create a variety of different meanings. No technique has the same meaning in all the different instances in which it occurs. A close-up can suggest emotional intimacy, or it can create fear and alarm, or it can open a window on character psychology.

Consider a close-up from *The Third Man* (1949), a film about corruption in post-WWII Vienna. This character is part of a criminal ring that sells diluted penicillin to hospitals; children die as a result. The close-up, which is slightly askew because the camera is canted (turned slightly to one side), tells us something about his moral nature, and it infers that that he is somehow twisted and shady. It will not surprise us later to learn that he is quite corrupt.

Contrast that image with the close-up from *The Gold Diggers*

FIGURE XII *The Third Man*. A slightly canted close-up used to make a character seem ominous.

of 1933 (1933), a musical that depicts down-and-out people striving and succeeding through pluck, energy, and talent. Notice how the light on the woman's face makes her seem luminous. It would be hard to think ill of her, and harder still to think her capable of anything but virtuous action. She is about to sing a song that consists of a plea for help for unemployed army veterans.

In these images, we see the same technique but two quite different meanings.

Now let's look at two long shots. The first is an image from the opening sequence of *On the Waterfront* (1954). Like the image from *The Third Man*, it depicts evil men, but notice how the long shot makes the men seem to be overwhelmed by their surroundings. They seem less sinister than the fellow in *The Third Man*. Many of them are corrupt union officials, but the film seems to be making a very different statement about their moral characters. The image suggests that they are dwarfed by their social context, the huge visual landscape that seems more powerful than they. Rather than being naturally evil like the character in *The Third Man*, the shot seems to suggest that immoral people may be shaped by their environment. Perhaps they are victims of circumstance and can be redeemed; they are not inherently bad.

As with the close-up, however, the meaning of a long

FIGURE XIII *The Gold Diggers of 1933.* A close-up used to make a character seem worthy of sympathy.

FIGURE XIV *On the Waterfront.* A long shot used to suggest the influence of social environment on moral character.

FIGURE XV *The Conformist.* A long shot used to suggest a character has no moral stature because he conforms too much to the conservative world around him.

shot will not be the same in all movies. If the long shot from *On the Waterfront* implies hope for the characters by suggesting they are victims of their environment, this one from *The Conformist* (1970) makes its main character seem a hopeless traitor to human values. He is on his way to betray a close friend and former teacher to the conservative Fascist government of Italy in the 1920s. The director, Bernardo Bertulucci, deliberately shoots him in such a way that he appears to have the moral substance of an ant. His debt to his environment, his "conformism," is in this instance a reason for blame rather than an excuse for bad actions.

FIGURE XVI *The Philadelphia Story.* The Greek columns suggest wealth and upper-class life.

The same lesson—that a technique has multiple possible uses and meanings—holds for all aspects of filmmaking, from props to colors to costumes to sets. A classic Greek column might be a metaphor for "the rule of law" in one movie (*12 Angry Men*; 1957), but in another, the same Greek column might suggest wealth

FIGURE XVII *12 Angry Men.* The Greek columns of a courthouse are a metaphor for the rule of law.

and upper-class life (*The Philadelphia Story*; 1940).

It is important in doing film analysis that you remain flexible and open to the multiple semantic possibilities of film technique. There is no dictionary of symbols that explains what a single cinematic device will mean in every situation or context. In one context, columns mean one thing, but in a different film or a different context, they will mean something quite different. Any one device can mean a multiplicity of things. It all depends on how and where it is used.

It is also important to bear in mind that meaning is complex. Most movies mean several different things at once. *The Philadelphia Story* is about relations between men and women in mid-20th century America. It also is about how the American economy functioned at the time, creating an upper crust of super-wealthy, leisure class people. It is about Republican culture, which treasured virtues like honor and industry and feared falls from grace that ruined reputations. It concerns American journalism and how it easily succumbed to gossip. At another level of interpretation, it is about gender identity, about how women especially were being instructed to behave by a culture largely run by men.

And it refers to familiar literary forms such as the romance in which characters depart from reality, enter a dream state where anything is possible, and emerge enlightened in some way, having learned to be more flexible in their real lives as a result of the dream.

The Philadelphia Story is a fairly simple movie, and yet it has a lot of different possible meanings. The same is true of pretty much any film.

In conducting film analysis and in writing about film for your courses, you should learn to trust your own interpretive abilities. Filmmakers would not do certain things with technique in their films if they did not make sense to people like you. They do them precisely because they know we in the audience will probably feel and think in response to them as they intend us to feel and think. So trust your own insights. They are probably true or they probably get at what a film is about in some way. Just remember that there are multiple perspectives on a film. You may see a film about economics, but someone else will see the same film as being about gender identity. You are probably both right. A good rule in interpreting film is to leave yourself open to alternatives. Meaning is multiple, and all the inferences and implications of any one movie would be difficult to exhaust.

The purpose of this book is to equip you with skills that will allow you to transform your own insights into a persuasive vocabulary for class discussion and for paper writing. The next two sections will introduce you to shot analysis and to writing about film.

SHOT-BY-SHOT ANALYSIS

The kind of analysis you will be learning in this book is called shot-by-shot analysis. In such analysis, you describe techniques used in a series of shots or images of a film sequence, and you explicate the meaning of the techniques.

Here is a list of basic terms you will need to know to describe shots and to analyze movies. We've arranged them so that they correspond to the chapter divisions that follow.

1. **COMPOSITION**   The arrangement of elements within the frame of the image.

   Blocking   The arrangement of characters on the set and within the frame.

   Depth of field   The visible space that is kept in focus in front and behind the plane of vision in a shot.

   Field of vision   What one sees from the camera, which is different from the place or setting in which the film story occurs. Related to **Depth of field**, the amount of space that is in focus in an image. An object in focus in the deep background of a shot has a more expansive field of vision, while an object in focus closer to a camera has a more shallow field of vision.

   Foreground / Background   Terms to describe the spaces within the frame that are either distant from the camera or close to it. Usually, the foreground is between the camera and the actors and the background is behind the actors.

   Frame / Framing   The border of the image which demarcates the space of the action. The frame also creates the visual space of the image and is an important element of meaning because it selects, limits, and expands what can be seen and what contributes to meaning. Framing can be **loose** or **tight**, distant from the object filmed or close to it. Framing can also be **open** or **closed**. In a closed frame, visual space is visible around the elements, while in an open frame, one of the elements extends beyond the line of the frame.

Mise-en-scène A French term from theater that refers to the arrangement of elements (characters, props, set, space) within the frame of the image.

Negative space Empty space that has significance because of its relationship to the other objects in the frame, especially characters.

Pro-filmic space The space in front of the camera within the frame of the image.

Visual plane Most shots contain a single visual plane, a point where focus occurs. All in front and all behind is out of focus. Some images in "deep focus photography" contain several visual planes because focus occurs at two or three different points.

2. **CINEMATOGRAPHY** The art of photographing a film.

    Shot One constant recording of events by a camera.

    Types of shot:

    Aerial shot An extreme high-angle shot from a helicopter or an airplane.

    Arc shot A continuous take that moves the camera in a circle around a character or an action.

    Close-up shot When the camera is close to the object so that the object takes up most of the space within the frame. Related to **Extreme close-up**, when the camera is placed at an unusually close distance from the object filmed.

    Crane shot As you would expect, a shot—usually high angle and sometimes mobile, as in the famous opening shot of *Touch of Evil*—from a crane.

    Dolly shot A shot made from a moving platform with wheels.

    Establishing shot Usually at the start of a sequence, it usually consists of a wide or full shot that tells the audience where the action about to be viewed occurs.

    Eye-level shot A shot taken at eye level.

    Handheld shot Filming done with a camera not mounted on a tripod.

    High-angle shot When the camera looks down at the object filmed. An **Extreme high-angle shot** exaggerates the effect by filming from an even greater height.

    Master shot A shot of the entire set and of all the characters, that is used to make sure that all the action is covered in the resulting takes.

    Medium shot A shot of characters from a medium distance.

    Long or Wide shot A shot that includes more of the environment and that usually includes all of the subject filmed.

    Pan shot A shot in which the camera rotates on its pivot but does not itself move in relation to the object. Also **Swish pan,** a fast pan that blurs the image as the camera swivels from one point to the next.

POV shot   A shot from the perspective of a character.

Reaction shot   A shot that cuts away from the action to show a character's reaction to the action.

Tilt shot   Angling the camera up or down on the action.

Tracking shot   When the camera moves, often on tracks or a truck, to follow the movement of an object.

Wide shot (also an **Extreme long shot**)   A shot from a great distance from the action, so that the ratio between figure and ground (landscape or set) is extreme.

Other terms from cinematography:

Camera distance   The space between the camera and the object filmed.

Canting   When the camera is tilted to make the object filmed appear at an angle.

Compositing   Creating a single image from a number of images filmed separately.

Deep focus   Deep focus lenses allow for greater depth of field, so that the background and the foreground can be simultaneously in focus.

Diffusion   A soft effect created by a filter.

Projection (Front and Rear)   Filming against a background onto which images are projected.

Rack focus   A sudden change of focal point from one visual plane to another, as when an object in the foreground ceases to be in focus while an object in the background comes into focus.

Soft focus   A blurring of the image achieved using filters or focal length adjustment.

Subjective camera or shot   The filming of the action from the perspective or point of view of a character. Related called a **Point of view (POV) shot.**

Two shot   A shot of two people.

Wide angle   The effect created by a lens with a shorter than normal focal length that allows a greater area to be filmed. Objects close to the camera appear larger and those far away smaller.

Zoom   Zooms move from a distance continuously to be close to an object, or move from close to an object to be far from it (zoom in, zoom out). This is achieved by changing the focal length of the camera's lens between wide angle and telephoto.

3. **EDITING**   The joining together of shots and series of shots to make a complete film.

   Continuity   Editing that matches action and objects from one sequence of images to the next so that the story is told continuously and no breaks occur in the visual flow.

Cut   The transition from one shot to the next. Includes **Crosscutting** and **Inter-cutting.** In crosscutting, two simultaneous and related actions are depicted, and the film cuts back and forth between them—as when in a chase, one character pursues and another is pursued. Inter-cutting is the insertion of a piece of film from another action in the middle of a sequence.

Cutaway   A shot that breaks an ongoing flow of matching shots by depicting a relevant detail that is connected to the on-going action.

Dissolve   The blending of one image into the next at a cut. Also called **Lap dissolve,** which is short for "overlap dissolve."

Exposition   The telling of the film story, usually by providing information about characters, settings, and issues.

Eyeline match   When the editing joins shots in which the eyelines of characters are at the same distance from the top of the frame from one shot to the next.

Fade (in or out)   When a shot or sequence begins or ends by slowly dissolving the image or by slowly bringing it into view.

Jump-cut   An abrupt transition through cutting that disturbs continuity.

Long take   A shot that is held for longer than normal amount of time without cutting.

Match cut   A cut that emphasizes continuity by matching one image with the image that follows, often by using the same eyeline.

Montage   A dynamic editing style that combines many shots, often rapidly, to make a point (about, say, the passage of time or the evolution of a character).

Parallel editing   Similar to crosscutting in that two simultaneous actions are linked by cutting back and forth between them. Crosscutting concerns simultaneous actions, and parallel editing usually implies a relationship of similarity at the level of meaning.

Reverse angle shot   A shot that reverses the perspective of a preceding shot. Often used in dialog and called **Shot reverse shot** to name the switching back and forth between interlocutors.

4. **ART DIRECTION (ALSO KNOWN AS PRODUCTION DESIGN)**   The design of the film in terms of setting, sound, lighting, and costume.

Chiaroscuro   An effect created by blurring light and dark and making objects lose their clear outline.

CGI   Computer generated imagery.

Diegetic sound   Sound that emerges from the action on the screen. **Nondiegetic sound** does not emerge from the screen action. Often this consists of an orchestral score and is called **Background music.** Related are **Synchronous** and **Nonsynchronous sound.** The first is sound that emerges from the action and accurately represents or matches it. The second is sound that is not matched to the image. Nonsynchronous sound often occurs at **sound bridges** between scenes, when sound from one carries over into another.

Exposure   The amount of light permitted to strike the film stock creating either dense, dark images (underexposed) or crisp, bright images (overexposed).

Filter   A cover on a lens that regulates the amount and kind of light hitting the film stock. Diffusion filters blur images, while polarizing filters increase contrast.

High-key lighting   When light fully illuminates the set bringing the objects filmed to a brilliant clarity of outline. Related to **Low-key lighting** which under-lights a set to create shadows and less clarity of vision.

Matte   An image created by combining two different shots of two different sets that are then combined to create the impression of a single set.

Saturation / Desaturation   Saturated color has more hue such as red or blue. Desaturated color is less strong and contains more white coloration. The color in an image can be saturated or desaturated. Saturation refers to the intensity of the color and to the dominance of hue. Saturated images tend to be vibrant and bright, while desaturated images are more muted.

Three Point Lighting   Used to create a realist effect that eliminates shadows, this technique uses three lights. A **key light** illuminates the characters; a **fill light** eliminates shadows; and a **back light** fills in the space between the characters and the back of the set.

5. **NARRATIVE**   The way the film story is told. Each narrative is differentiated according to point of view, tone, and style.

   Diegesis   The term used to name the story depicted on screen—as opposed to the story in real life time that the screen narrative is about.

   Sequence   A part of a film's narrative that records a complete action or event from beginning to end.

   Perspective   The point from which the action in a film is depicted or from which the story is told. For example, *Avatar* is told almost exclusively from Jake Scully's point of view. We follow his story and see his life. We see the world pretty much as he sees it, and this is brought home to us in numerous **point of view shots** that look over his shoulder at what he sees.

   Transition   A changeover in a narrative from one state of being to another. Transitions often take the form of reversals. An action that appeared headed in one direction turns in another quite different one.

6. **STYLE**   Style is a particular way of using film technique to represent the world. It varies in terms of technique (from cool to warm colors, for example) and in terms of theme (from the transparent realism of a romantic comedy to the dark images of a crime film about treachery and betrayal).

In doing shot-by-shot analysis of a film sequence, you should start by describing each shot in terms of camera position and angle: for example, downward tilt medium shot or high-angle long shot. After saying what kind of shot you see, describe the elements within the image and how they are arranged in relation to one another. Next, describe technical elements such as lighting, set, costume, props, colors, and the like. Some images are darker than others for a reason, while some use colors to suggest moral states. Next, describe the idea in the image and how it connects with other ideas or arguments made in the movie.

Let's start by considering a single image from a movie. This is an image from *The Best Years of Our Lives*, which was one of the most popular films of 1946. It won seven Academy Awards, including one for Best Film. It is the story of three veterans of World War II who have difficulty adjusting to home life. One of them, Al, was a lowly enlisted man in the Army but at home he is a wealthy banker. He gets into a conflict with his boss at the bank, Mr. Milton, because he feels veterans should be given loans to start small businesses, even if they have no collateral.

In this image, Al returns to work for the first time. It is a medium shot, and it is composed in such a way that the space in the frame is distributed unevenly. There is no symmetry, order, or harmony between its parts. Rather, there is unevenness between the two men. The image has two planes—a foreground, where Mr. Milton sits, and a background, where Al sits. Notice that Al seems much smaller than Mr. Milton. He is in fact taller, but the filmmakers obviously wanted to make a point about his comparative stature in relation to his boss. He has less power at the bank. He might fight for the rights of veterans, but the

FIGURE XVIII *The Best Years of Our Lives.* The placement of characters suggests their relative social power and their power in relation to one another.

ultimate right to decide rests with Mr. Milton. That idea is also embodied in the different spatial weight of each figure in the image. Mr. Milton has more space. He dominates the image visually just as he dominates Al hierarchically within the bank.

Now, let's consider several more images from the same movie. In addition to Al, there are two other veterans—Fred and Homer. Homer is a middle-class boy who lost both hands in combat and lives off a government disability pension. While Al was a lowly grunt in the army but a wealthy banker at home, Fred was a decorated Air Force Captain, but he comes from a working-class background and has trouble finding work that is not degrading. By making Fred superior to Al in the military and inferior to him in civilian life, the filmmakers suggest that people's real worth has nothing to do with social status or class location. That prepares for the film's argument that we are all equal members of a community. Because of this, we have an obligation, like that of an individual soldier in an army platoon, to help each other. The movie argues that veterans, especially poor ones without financial resources, deserve help. They are worthy of it because they have inner value apart from their class location and social status. Their collateral is what is inside them.

This image is a close medium shot of Al speaking to a veteran who wants a loan, but who has no collateral. This composition resembles the one in the previous image, only now Al is in Mr. Milton's position in the foreground, and he is larger in the frame. But notice that this image is composed differently. The veteran, though he is in the seemingly subordinate position in the background, actually seems larger than Al because he occupies more space. Does this suggest that he has more value than Al? That seems doubtful, given how the movie endorses the idea that we are all equal, an idea suggested by the dark line across the screen that links the two men. The composition probably is meant to suggest the man has as much value or worth as Al, despite the fact that he owns no property.

Notice how the actors have been instructed to behave. Al looks away, thinking about the veteran's request for a loan to start a vegetable farm like the one he had in the Army that helped feed his fellow soldiers. The veteran is a natural farmer, but he can't qualify for a loan because he lacks collateral. Notice how the veteran and Al are matched in a parallel in the frame. Both lean to the right almost in harmony, and both are wearing matching dark suits. The visual image seems to imply sympathy between the two. So why does Al look away? That look probably conveys the idea that he is troubled by the fact that he has to follow bank rules that would deny the man a loan, yet he respects this man and appreciates his worth. The image implies the idea of this conflict visually. The lines on the set in the background are strikingly rigid and orderly, like the inflexible rules of the bank Al has to contend with. Both Al and the veteran seem to bend away from those straight lines, as if what is needed here is a bit more flexibility on the part of the bank, a bending of its rules.

In the next image, a cooler, more distant medium shot than the last close-up, Al, having decided to give the veteran a loan, is criticized for doing so by Mr. Milton, his boss in the bank. Normally, you would expect Al to

FIGURE XX *The Best Years of Our Lives*. A character is situated in the center of the frame to suggest his greater moral stature.

be a subordinate figure in an image representing such an event. The shot is composed more loosely than the last, creating greater dept of field and drawing in more rigid-looking elements from the set in the background, and that seems appropriate for a situation in which someone is being reminded of the fact that he is part of an institution whose rules he has not followed. The medium shot emphasizes the room as opposed to the people's personalities in it. Rules are part of an institution that supposedly transcends personal relations between people.

But notice that Al is not a subordinate figure in the image. He is dead center, and he is standing. Of the two other people in the room, one is lower in the frame and off to the side. He also occupies much less space. The other character to the far left, a bank official, has been directed to stand a bit further back in comparison to Al, so that in the image, he looks smaller, and this gives rise to a slight triangle. The apex of the triangular composition of elements in the frame is Al's head. Although Al has broken bank rules, one gets the feeling from this image that he has done the right thing in the eyes of the filmmakers. The men who are critical of him are either lower than him or off to the side in relation to him. Significantly, one of them is Mr. Milton, the bank director who was so much larger than Al in the first image we looked at.

Shot-by-shot analysis thus begins with a description of the image on the screen using the technical vocabulary of filmmaking (medium shot, composition, depth of field, etc.). It then moves to a discussion of the various components of the image, from set to character relationships to composition. And then it moves to a description of the ideas in the images—what they might mean.

Now let's consider a more complicated example from *The Best Years of Our Lives*. Each of the three veterans has difficulty adjusting to civilian life. Homer, the sailor who lost both hands and who wears prosthetic devices instead, can't adjust at all and has difficulty reestablishing his old romantic relationship with Wilma, the girl next door. Fred loses his wife and his job, and Al returns to wars at work and alcoholism. In this sequence the three ride in a taxi, returning to their home town for the first time since going away to war. Their life in the military provided them with a community of rough equals who cared for one another. As they ride in the back of a taxi together, they look forward to their new life, but they are also anxious and look back toward the comfortable community of men in which they have lived for the past four years. They look out on images of mothers with children and the new commercial boom of the postwar period.

The first image of the sequence is a medium close-up of the men in the back of the taxi. Notice how a horizontal compositional line across the image is made up of their heads, emphasizing their equality. No one is made to seem superior or better. The tight framing is also important because it makes it appear as if they also form a community, which is suggested by their co-presence within the same image in so confined a space. This is the norm of companionable male fellowship in the military that they are leaving behind. They are about to enter a world of frustrated vocational hopes, unequal economic relations, and troubled personal attachments. As you might expect, the filmmakers try to communicate this reality in images characterized by imbalance and asymmetry that lack harmony or unity. Already this image has an element of negativity about it. It embodies their fears and anxieties. The men are in a cramped visual space, as if the world around them may be threatening. The men seem contained within the image in a way that is both comforting and close but also hemmed in.

The second image of the sequence is a subjective long shot facing out at the street from the men's point of view. The camera position thus aligns the audience with them and with their feelings. But the looser framing and the wider angle of vision create a new sense of negativity. Notice that it is a non-symmetrical image that creates a huge inequality between the size of the men (in the tiny rear-view mirror of the taxi) and the world outside the taxi. Why would the filmmakers want to make such a negative, even scary image? It makes the world they are about to enter seem alien and distant, but perhaps that is a good way of representing their feelings of hope and fear about what they are about to encounter after having been away for four years. Much may have changed, and they don't

FIGURE XXI *The Best Years of Our Lives.* The three veterans, each from a different social class, look like equals in this composition.

FIGURE XXII *The Best Years of Our Lives*. The image depicts the men's anxiety at the idea of returning home after several years of absence. Notice how small they appear in rear view mirror and how dark much of the image is.

know how they will fit in. In comparison to the houses outside, the men seem very small indeed in the mirror. That tiny image seems to remind us of how small they feel as they confront a world that is both familiar and alien.

When they arrive at Homer's house, he suggests going out for a drink, but the others order him out of the taxi. Seen in a loosely framed medium shot from their point of view, he emerges into the world he left behind. The camera placement within the car seems to further the sense that Homer is still linked to the community of men. Notice the prominence of the car in the framing. He is not yet beyond its comforting embrace.

In the next image, the camera shifts to the point of view of the house and to a long shot that creates a greater sense of distance between the house and Homer. The image seems to communicate his alienation, his feeling of non-belonging. A small detail, the metalwork grill on the door, adds an element of negativity, a kind of bar to access to his old world. It is far from being a warm and welcoming composition. The house is pictured as he sees it, as a closed, unwelcoming, even emotionally dangerous place, and his smallness in relation to it embodies his feelings of trepidation and anxiety.

In the next, shot, the camera assumes Homer's perspective in a loosely framed medium shot. Homer stands stock-still as his sister runs out of the house, shouts, runs to a neighbor's house, and runs back. The camera pans to

FIGURE XXIII *The Best Years of Our Lives*. Homer exits the taxi, but the perspective of the camera lingers with the other men.

FIGURE XXIV *The Best Years of Our Lives*. This shot from the house captures Homer's fears about how he will be received.

follow her. In the midst of all the motion and commotion, Homer's stillness is striking.

The next shot repeats the earlier image from inside the taxi. Homer is hugged by his sister, and his parents run out to greet him. At this point, the music swells upward to match the emotional elevation the reunion achieves. But this warm image is again undermined by the coldness of the taxi door. Something is wrong, and we don't quite know what it is yet, but the shot from inside the taxi seems to tell us something. Perhaps part of Homer is still there, still caught up in his experiences in the war. It is possible he has not quite gotten out of the taxi yet. Emotionally, he may still be stuck in the past.

We get a better sense of how that inability to overcome his past may affect his life in the next shot. A medium shot, again, like all of these, it is located behind Homer and his parents. Notice that the cinematographer has deliberately pushed them to the far left side of the image. Why? Well, it opens up a great gap or distance between that side of the image and the other side, where Homer's old girlfriend, Wilma, is coming out of her house to greet him. Notice how much distance the filmmakers have deliberately created between them, using a wide angle and loose framing. It is a visual correlate of the estrangement between Homer and his girlfriend. He has been away for four years; he has been horribly wounded. We get a sense from the visual arrangement of this

FIGURE XXV *The Best Years of Our Lives.* The camera pans to follow Homer's sister as she celebrates his return. The shot contrasts her freedom of movement with his emotional immobility.

FIGURE XXVI *The Best Years of Our Lives*. An unexpected shot from inside the taxi suggests Homer is still caught in the past.

FIGURE XXVII *The Best Years of Our Lives*. Space is used now as a visual device to comment on the emotional distance that separates Homer from a successful reunion with his old girlfriend.

image of just how hard a time he will have rediscovering himself and reestab-lishing his old relationships. But there is something else going on here from the point of view of cinematography. The filmmakers have used a deep focus lens that allows both Homer and his girlfriend to be in focus at the same time. It seems to connect them even as the space suggests difficulty. And it adds an element of hope.

His girlfriend emerges from her house, and we have a first close-up. She is associated by the shot with greater intimacy and with the possibility of a successful personal relationship. But Homer is not ready to embrace that intimacy just yet.

When he is hugged by his girlfriend in the next shot, a medium shot that draws his entire family into the frame, he cannot raise his arms (both lost in battle and replaced by hooks), and the meaning of his immobility becomes clearer. His visual immobility suggests emotional rigidity, and that will be his greatest handicap. He is unable to connect with others, to accept their help, and to move forward in life. The placement of the camera behind him reinforces the sense of a lack of emotional openness, a failure to be honest with himself and with others about his feelings regarding his handicap.

This analysis of each image would need to be amplified to encompass the entire argument of the film. How does this sequence fit into the argument of the movie as a whole? The film depicts the troubles of veterans of World War II,

FIGURE XXVIII   *The Best Years of Our Lives*. A close-up suggests the possibility of emotional renewal for Homer.

FIGURE XXIX *The Best Years of Our Lives.* Homer remains stock still in this medium shot, unable to hug his girlfriend and unable, just yet, to successfully re-enter his home world.

and by choosing men from three different class backgrounds, it suggests that the three classes in American society can be harmonious with each other. It is critical of the business community for not being helpful enough to returning veterans. It argues that the wealthy needs to do more to foster economic opportunity for those without wealth. This sequence furthers that larger argument by using point-of-view shots to place the audience in the perspective of the veterans. Those shots force us to see the world as they see it. That makes it easier to empathize with them. This sequence thus furthers the argument of the film by making the audience appreciate more concretely the kinds of problems veterans of World War II faced.

WRITING ABOUT FILM: THE ART OF ACTIVE VIEWING

When we watch movies for entertainment, it is for fun, and we never take notes. When we watch films with a scholarly eye, it is active viewing; we watch, reflect, take notes, and analyze.

Film analysis is usually called "criticism." Criticism does not mean "disparagement." While we may have negative reactions when we are writing analytically and critically about films, we are primarily making claims about the film's meaning using evidence from the film. To write critically requires that one distance oneself from the text. Rather than be involved in whether or not a character will succeed, one studies the character objectively and asks how the character is constructed, what function he or she serves in the film's design, and how he or she embodies ideas about the world.

Writing critically about film often means watching the film more than once. The first time we watch a film we may behave as any other audience member—albeit one paying particularly close attention and taking occasional notes. The next time we watch a film, we may try to think like a filmmaker; ask how the film is put together, how a filmmaker might justify filming the action in a certain way instead of another. We watch with an eye for textual analysis—how are film techniques being used? How is the narrative constructed? What types of values does the filmmaker appear to be promoting and how?

Here are some helpful guides for writing critically about movies.

Ask yourself why the filmmakers did something a particular way. Why is the camera where it is? Why are certain colors being used? Why does the image look as it does? Try to determine what idea the filmmakers had in mind when they constructed an image in a particular way. How does the way the image is made relate to the characters in the film? Or to the issues and conflicts that move the plot forward?

Practice writing while you watch movies. It's important to get into the habit of taking notes while watching films. Film scholars watch the texts that they're studying many times over, but unfortunately we don't always have time for multiple viewings in the limited space between class periods. One way to make up for this is by taking careful screening notes. Some important things to take down: the title and director, names of main characters and their relationships, setting (geographical and chronological), and major narrative points and events. If you miss any of these main points, consider using a site such as the Internet Movie Database (www.imdb.com) to fill in the gaps.

You should also develop a shorthand for film techniques such as the medium shot (MS) or the close-up (CU), as well as the major angles such as high angle (HA) and movements such as the pan shot (PS).

In your critical essays, try to avoid the language of movie reviews. Evaluations of "greatness" have no place in critical writing. Your duty is to understand, not to evaluate. Also, try not to speculate or to judge. Certainly a film could have ended differently, a character might have changed her fate by behaving more logically, and one could ask if these events might have really happened in real life. But for our purposes here, such questions and concerns should be put aside.

Keep your audience in mind. For whom are you writing? Typically your writing is for your professor and perhaps your classmates. They're probably familiar with the film that you're writing about. You can therefore forgo long summaries of the plot and the history of the director's career, unless the professor says otherwise. In writing on *Iron Man*, for example, you should not give a detailed summary of the movie, but you should concentrate instead on the plot details necessary to explain your points about the film. Tony Stark is a billionaire; he has an awkward relationship with his personal assistant; he feels guilty about the impact his arms dealings have had in Afghanistan; he has a romantic fling with a magazine writer. Any one of these pieces of information might be necessary to explain a thesis statement, but it's unlikely that they would all be necessary in a short analytical paper on the film.

In writing critically, choose an aspect of the film that interests you, such as the use of color or the theme of betrayal or the way a particular character is portrayed. For example, American businessmen are portrayed very differently in *Avatar* and *Iron Man*. What difference does that make? Criticism, as you'll notice in the second half of this book, covers a range of concerns, from psychology and politics to history and even science.

In writing critically, you should also justify the point you wish to make about a movie by referring to specific aspects of the film or to moments in the film that substantiate your claim. Describe a particular shot or sequence. Try to avoid making very general statements that you do not back up with evidence.

In thinking critically and analytically about a film, you should break it down into parts—shots, editing, composition, lighting, set, characters, etc. Try to determine how the different pieces work together to make meaning.

Critical papers often follow a familiar five-part format. In the first part, you lay out the point you want to make. In the next three parts, you offer evidence to support your point—usually citing at least three different parts of a movie very specifically and concretely. And, in the final part, you bring the different strands of your argument together and reach a conclusion regarding the film.

For example, a critical essay on "The use of color in Jean-Pierre Jeunet's *Amelie*" might begin in this way:

> Jean-Pierre Jeunet's *Amelie* operates like a painting in which the colors used to depict the world are as important as what is depicted. The colors that stand out most in the film are green, red, and orange. Settings such as subway stations that might in a realist film have appeared to be dingy, dirty, and grey instead appear in this movie to glow with a deeply saturated green. Characters who might normally be expected to wear costumes with a range of colors instead wear clothing that is almost always the same two basic colors, red and green. I will argue that green is a color that suggests latency, much as the green of plants points to the possibility of life held in check, not yet in blossom, while red suggests the possibility of a passionate engagement with life. In the course of the film, Amelie must move from green to red if she is to overcome her fears, to become less introverted, and to make contact with the man she loves. If green suggests calm self-containment, red in the film is associated with taking risks, with the possibility of romance, and with opening oneself more to the world around one. And what you get when you mix the two is orange, a color one character associates with successful romantic relationships. It is the color that dominates the film's final images.

FIGURES XXXI & XXXII   *Amelie*. Director Jean-Pierre Jeunet lays out his color palette: red, green, orange.

This introductory paragraph lays out an idea about the film, and it refers to the way cinematic technique (in this case, production design) works in the movie to further the film's themes. It does not yet substantiate or justify the writer's claim regarding the movie by referring to specific images. That working out of the argument takes place in the next few paragraphs. Here is one such possible paragraph:

The colors red and green are in balance throughout the film, but one color usually is dominant in certain scenes. Amelie's home contains elements of both colors, but red is dominant because Amelie, although she leads a shy and introverted life, harbors secret passions within her. When she is most shy and introverted, she wears green, a color that suggests calmness, self-control, and an absence of passion. But it is also the color of nature and of the potential for growth, and that is clear in its association with Amelie's father, a man who must learn, like her, to take chances, to leave home, and to explore the world. He is depicted standing next to a garden gate that makes his home resemble a prison, and his backyard garden, where he spends a lot of time, is overwhelmingly green. Like him, Amelie is reticent and shy, and she often wears green. But she also wears red when she is arranging a romantic relationship for Joseph and Georgette, two lonely, inept people, and she is in red when she meets Nino, the man she is destined to fall in love with. They encounter each other first in the Abbesses metro station, and it is important that the station is touched up in post-production to look very green. But it is important that Amelie wears red as she walks through the station. She bears within her the potential for a passionate blossoming, an idea confirmed by the advertisements on the wall of the station which consist of images of orange fruit. During this scene, a blind man plays a love song, and the metaphoric comparison with Amelie herself is clear. She too is blind to the possibilities of romance around her, even as she harbors romantic possibilities and longings within herself. A few moments later, of course, having followed the sound of the love song to the blind man sitting under images of fruit, she meets Nino for the first time. All three of the film's primary colors—green, red, and orange—are present in this scene.

FIGURES XXXIII & XXXIV *Amelie.* Amelie and Nino on either side of a door that is green on one side and red on the other.

After several paragraphs like this one that lay out evidence from the film to justify the argument of the essay, you should conclude with a paragraph that sums up your observations and your thoughts about the movie. Here is one possible way of doing it:

> In *Amelie*, color correlates not just with mood but also with existential condition. Some people, the film suggests, are afraid of the world. Like Defayel, the man of glass, they hide away, never going out, painting the same picture over and over again, following routines and habits that protect them from chance encounters and from contact with existence but that simultaneously deprive them of life. Like green plants that never blossom into colorful blooms, they lead a latent life. Amelie also lives a green life of latency, while longing for a full flowered existence. This chromatic duality codifies the interaction between Nino and Amelie in the scene in which they finally connect romantically near the end of the film. They are separated by a door against which each places a cheek. On Amelie's side, the door is red, on Nino's side green. When Nino enters her apartment, he leaves green behind, and they both finally are on the side of red. Their communication up to this point has always been mediated by signs such as notes and photographs, things that represent reality but are not reality itself. Now, as Nino begins to speak (to use the mediation of signs once again), Amelie asks him to be quiet and to make physical contact instead. The two lovers cross from latency to fulfillment in their personalities and in their relationship, and they also cross from distance and separation in regard to life to active engagement and real physical contact with it. Throughout the film, Jeunet elaborates this theme in terms of the colors red and green, but now the mix of the two—orange—makes its grand appearance after a number of earlier allusions. At one point, a character refers to love as an orange day, and orange lies, of course, between red and green on the color spectrum. Fittingly, the film concludes with Amelie and Nino riding a motor scooter through Paris on a very orange looking day.

FIGURE XXXV *Amelie*. Amelie and Nino now combine red and green into orange.

The goal of this book is to teach you how better to analyze films, but bear in mind that thinking carefully about films—and writing critically about them—does not prohibit enjoyment of the movie-watching experience. You will soon discover that multiple, active viewings of a film will grant you deeper understanding of a film's meaning and of the cinematic techniques used to deliver it, as well as give you the opportunity to more carefully consider its role in our culture.

PART 1

Technique and Meaning

Composition

If you pause a movie, you see something resembling a photograph. The difference is that everything inside the movie image consists of artificially arranged elements that have been deliberately assembled to resemble real life. Little of what you see in a movie image is as a result accidental.

The composition of images is an important way for filmmakers to communicate ideas and tell a story. An important feature of any composed image is the placement of the frame. The frame can be close to the object filmed (tight) or far away (loose). Each creates a different semantic effect.

The image from *Mildred Pierce* (1945) is tightly framed, and there is very little empty space around the figures. The image draws on the limited frame

FIGURE 1.1 *Mildred Pierce.* The tight frame of the image is suited to the idea that Mildred's amoral urges are being contained by the law.

space of the Academy Ratio (1.35:1) to portray Mildred as trapped by representatives of the law. She has attempted to pin a murder on a friend in order
to protect her daughter, but she has also strayed from prevailing gender norms
by getting a divorce and becoming a successful businesswoman. She is being
constrained by the police for both "crimes."

In contrast, the loosely framed image from *The Searchers* (1956) creates a
very different meaning effect. It draws on the resources of the widescreen aspect
ration of 1.75:1 to create a feeling of a dangerous empty space around the
figures. The wide angle image embodies the movie's theme—that civilization is a
fragile construct whose institutions could easily be destroyed.

FIGURE 1.2 *The Searchers.* The widescreen frame format and the open frame allow empty space to be a more
pronounced element of meaning.

The arrangement of objects within the frame obeys certain common-sense
principles of valuation or inflection. A filmmaker usually assigns greater importance or value to characters who are centered within the frame or who are
located in the upper half of the image. Characters who are of less value or who
are subordinated in some way are often placed in the lower half or off to the
side. The lower half of the image generally serves the function of an adjective of
diminishment.

For example, in *The Heiress* (1949), a father and daughter disagree over
whom she should marry. The father is domineering, and he makes certain she
does not marry a man she loves because the father suspects, rightly, that the
man is a gold-digger who wants the girl's wealth. In the first image from early
on in the film, the father is centered and in the upper part of the screen. At this
point in the film, he is alerting his daughter to the danger she faces by marrying
someone who does not love her. His dominant position in her life is suggested
by his placement in the image. In the second image, from later in the film, the

daughter stands up to him. She accuses him of having stolen from her the one chance she had for a romantic relationship in her life. She is now in the upper half of the screen and he is in the lower half.

FIGURES 1.3 & 1.4 *The Heiress*. Composition depicts changing relations of power between a daughter and her domineering father.

The meaning of these common uses of space and location vary. It is not always the case that someone high in the frame has more power or value, or that someone lower has less. Sometimes a primary character will be placed off to the side to evoke pathos or empathy. In this image from *In the Mood for Love* (2000), for example, a character is placed in the lower left quadrant of the image. But this placement is not negative, nor is it a demotion in value. He has just learned his wife is having an affair with another man; he feels betrayed, and the seemingly negative placement is designed to evoke our sympathy for him.

FIGURE 1.5 *In the Mood for Love*. A character's suffering is suggested by his placement in the frame.

The placement of the character from *In the Mood for Love* is in keeping with cinematographers' preferences for placement within the image. According to cinematography's rule of thirds, if you divide an image into three parts both vertically and horizontally you will get four points where four squares intersect, and those are favored by cinematographers in their effort to design balanced and unified images.

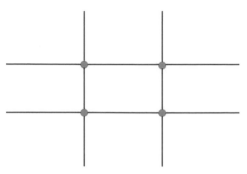

FIGURE 1.6 The rule of thirds in cinematography designates points within the frame that cinematographers favor.

Important characters can also be placed low in the frame to show that they are victims of injustice. In the image from *Enemy of the State* (1998), a man who is virtuous and who is about to be murdered is low in the frame. But in this instance, the positioning is meant to convey superiority. He is about to be harmed by the man to the left who looms over him in a threatening manner. In this instance, the fact that the man lower in the frame is centered in the image is more important than his inferior location.

FIGURE 1.7 *Enemy of the State*. A lower position in the frame evokes empathy.

In *12 Angry Men*, a positive character occupies both upper and lower positions in successive images. A single juror (#8) holds out for "Not Guilty" in a murder trial. Eventually, he convinces all of the other jurors, but the process is difficult and laced with conflict. In the early sequences, Juror #8 is depicted standing over the other jurors to suggest the rightness of his position, but he is also placed in a lower position within compositions early in the film to show how difficult his task is. Nevertheless, despite having other jurors standing over him, he is frequently centered to suggest the virtue of his position in comparison to theirs. They may dominate the visual space (and the argument), but one senses visually that he is right.

FIGURES 1.8 & 1.9 *12 Angry Men.* Placement within the frame often tells us visually who has virtue or power.

The way space is distributed in the image can also be used to make meaning. Characters can occupy different amounts of space in relation to one another. In *Before the Devil Knows You're Dead* (2007), Hank and Andy are brothers who need money and who decide to rob their parents' jewelry store. The robbery goes awry, and their mother is killed. Andy dominates Hank in this tale of betrayal within a family, and that fact is registered both by his superior position and by the greater amount of space he is assigned in this image.

FIGURE 1.10 *Before the Devil Knows You're Dead.* One character is assigned more space in the image to connote his dominance over the other.

Empty space is often used for semantic emphasis. In the image from *North Country* (2005), a film about the first lawsuit brought against a corporation for sexual harassment, a single mother, Josey Aimes, a female worker at a mine, sits in despair after being bullied by a male coworker. The imbalance between her small figure and the huge empty space around her does a good job of portraying the greater power of the corporation in relation to her. She has been made to feel small, and the unbalance between figure and space in the frame provides a perfect correlate for her emotional state.

FIGURE 1.11 *North Country*. Negative space augments the character's sense of alienation and anguish at this point in the film.

Composition also relies on visual planes such as foreground and background. In this image from the beginning of *Bicycle Thieves* (1948), an Italian Neorealist film, Antonio and Maria are a poor married couple who live in a crowded tenement outside Rome in the immediate aftermath of World War II. Antonio gets a job hanging movie posters, but he can't afford a bicycle. Maria makes a sacrifice and gives up her treasured wedding linen to get the needed money. In the image, Maria places a heavy bucket of water on the table in the foreground while Antonio stands in the background. The way she is foregrounded in the composition alerts the viewer that her virtues of silent endurance and hard work will provide her husband with the assistance he needs.

Placing characters in the background of the image makes them smaller, and that easily correlates with moral demotion. In *Before the Devil Knows You're Dead*, for example, Sidney Lumet has Hank move into the deep background of the frame as he goes to tell his brother that he agrees to help commit a crime. He doesn't know yet that the crime will consist of robbing their parents' jewelry store, but the image construction alerts us to the fact that he is diminishing in stature in some way.

FIGURE 1.12 *Bicycle Thieves*. A wife's silent labor on behalf of her family is foregrounded, foreshadowing the enormous sacrifice she is about to make.

FIGURE 1.13 *Before the Devil Knows You're Dead*. A character walks to the back of the image as he loses moral stature.

FIGURE 1.14 *On the Waterfront*. A figure in the background is the center of attention and the point of greatest value.

Being small and in the background of an image is not necessarily a bad thing. We are not supposed to think less of Antonio because he stands in the deep background of the image from *Bicycle Thieves*. Similarly, in *On the Waterfront*, the hero in this image is depicted as a small figure in the background. But notice how all the other characters are turned towards him as he departs. They are all members of a corrupt union, and the direction of the composition formed by them is aimed at him. He may be in the background but he is the center of visual and social attention. He is the hero of the film, and this early image suggests that he has moral qualities that separate him from his cronies. His positioning in the background is thus a positive accent.

The composition of elements within the frame can be either orderly and symmetrical or asymmetrical and uneven. Usually in symmetrical compositions, lines can be drawn between elements that are grouped together. Geometric shapes such as triangles often result. In this image from *Mildred Pierce*, Mildred's daughter is finally caught for the murder committed at the start of the film. The filmmakers want to convey the sense that order has finally been restored to the world, and they do so with a highly symmetrical composition.

FIGURE 1.15 *Mildred Pierce.* A triangular composition suggests a restoration of order.

While symmetrical composition would seem to lend itself to a sense of implied order in the world, it can also be qualified by conflict—a symmetrical balance between contending elements. And symmetry can also be used to depict negatively a social order that is too rigid, authoritarian, and unfair and that is imposed on people against their will.

In *The Philadelphia Story*, the story of a couple who divorce at the outset and are reunited in the end, Tracy is the haughty daughter of a wealthy family; Dexter is a likeable scoundrel who shows up on the day of her wedding to another man determined to wreck her plans and win her back. He succeeds. But, first, she has to learn to be less haughty and independent. In this symmetrical image, Dexter stands with Tracy's mother and younger sister. The compositional line formed by their heads suggests unity and harmony. We get the sense that Dexter stands a good chance of winning from the ease with which he blends back into the family community both visually and socially. In contrast, Tracy seems out of place and off to the side. Yet, while she is left out of one symmetry, there is another symmetry between the two equally balanced halves of the screen. Despite Tracy's exclusion from the community on the left side of the image, one sense from this image that ultimately this community will find a way to reunite.

FIGURE 1.16 *The Philadelphia Story*. Symmetry of composition.

While symmetry is used to depict what the filmmakers think are positive states in *The Philadelphia Story*, in *Paths of Glory* (1957), a socially critical film by Stanley Kubrick about World War I, symmetry plays a quite different role. In this film, common soldiers are mistreated by corrupt generals. The generals order an impossible attack that fails, and, to avoid taking the blame themselves, they decide several soldiers should be executed as a lesson to others. Their actions are portrayed negatively, and the rigid and inflexible character of military discipline is rendered in highly symmetrical images.

FIGURES 1.17 & 1.18 *Paths of Glory*. Symmetry is used to characterize the rigidity of military discipline.

Other film styles thrive on asymmetry. One such style is film noir ("black film"), a genre that was popular in the 1940s. It is called film noir because of the strong lighting contrasts often found in such films. But it is also a genre whose storylines are dominated by immorality, betrayal, duplicity, and murder, actions and qualities that are often characterized in this kind of film by non-traditional, usually asymmetrical, compositions.

In *Mildred Pierce*, from the classic era of film noir after World War II, Mildred is investigated by the police for a murder, but the film is also an investigation of her decision to divorce her husband and to set out alone in life as an independent businesswoman. Made at a time when women were being urged back into the home and more domestic identities after the war (during which women had taken men's jobs and worked in factories), the film depicts Mildred's independence as causing havoc in her world. She must be brought back into line by the police inspector. Asymmetrical compositions that grant him visual superiority to her are common during the police sequences.

FIGURE 1.19 *Mildred Pierce*. Asymmetrical compositions emphasize the film's project of bringing Mildred back into line with prevailing gender norms.

Some images combine both symmetry and asymmetry in their composition. In this image from *The Best Years of Our Lives*, Fred, a war hero from a poor background, tries to talk his way onto a regular commercial air flight so that he can return home after the war. But all flights are booked. In this image, he leans on the airline worker's desk and tries to cajole her into allowing him on a flight.

Behind him stands a black porter carrying the luggage and golf clubs of the well-to-do businessman who stands off to the left. The businessman has a reservation and can get on the flight, even though, the filmmakers suggest, he has led a life of recreation (golfing) while Fred has been away risking his life for his country. Notice how the filmmakers place Fred in the middle of a symmetrical line that runs from the female airline worker to the black porter standing behind Fred. They are a community of equals, all workers, and the line of symmetry both unites them and distinguishes them from the businessman, who stands apart to the left. He seems aloof from the visual community the three other characters form. He constitutes an asymmetrical element in the composition. This early image thus uses composition to stage an important conflict the film will explore between returning veterans who lack property and businessmen who possess wealth but are reluctant to lend it to veterans.

FIGURE 1.20 *The Best Years of Our Lives.* This image uses both symmetry and asymmetry to depict tensions in post-World War II America.

Contemporary filmmakers usually play symmetrical compositions off asymmetrical ones to convey meaning. In *A History of Violence* (2005), symmetry is used to characterize a fragile harmony that is founded on a lie, and asymmetry is used to depict the truth that the lie represses. A man who seems to be a family man and an upstanding citizen of his town turns out to be an urban criminal who has reinvented himself. Tom Stall is a liar, and gangsters from his past catch up with him and attempt to destroy his new life. Here, for example, is Tom's home life. Notice how he and his daughter are balanced at the center of the frame, while his wife and son are on either side, also balanced in a perfect symmetry. Their family is portrayed as a supportive one; they care for each other; and this spirit of care is juxtaposed to the violent dangers that lie just outside the range of their lives. When those dangers show up, notice how the composition changes. A gangster sits at the counter of Tom's café, while Tom's wife prepares coffee. The composition is asymmetrical; the gangster's form is large and dark while Tom's wife, much smaller in the frame, looks vulnerable in contrast.

FIGURES 1.21 & 1.22 *A History of Violence.* Symmetrical and asymmetrical compositions are used to depict a conflict between a man's aspirations for a normal family life and his criminal past.

Student Assignment: *12 Angry Men* (1.28.30 to 1.30.00)

Do a shot-by-shot analysis of the sequence. The title of the sequence might be "You're alone." How does the sequence of shots use composition to display the conflict between the jurors? The filmmakers clearly want you to take sides with Juror #8 (played by Henry Fonda). How do the compositions favor him? How do they portray his nemesis, the one remaining hold-out, Juror #3 (played by Lee. J. Cobb)?

Student Assignment: *Gaslight* (1944) (25:50 to 27:00)

Think about the ways Nancy and Gregory are framed compared to Paula. How is the frame divided and shared? Compare the ways Paula and Gregory are framed. How is each character placed? Consider the depth of field—with whom do you think the viewer is meant to empathize? How do you know? How are symmetry and asymmetry used in this sequence? What do we learn about the characters? What is left unknown? How does the composition of the sequence move the narrative forward?

Student Assignment: *The Royal Tenenbaums* (2001) (44:37 to 45:19)

How are the characters in this sequence framed? How would you describe the composition of these scenes? What strikes you as interesting or perplexing about the composition; what aspects are particularly noticeable? Why? What do we learn about the characters based on the composition of this sequence? How does the composition move the narrative forward? Does the composition of this sequence remind you of a famous work of art.

FIGURE 1.23 *The Royal Tenenbaums*. A carefully composed image gives every character a place in the frame.

FURTHER READING

Cossar, Harper. *Letterboxed: The Evolution of Widescreened Cinema*. Lexington: University of Kentucky Press, 2001.

Gibbs, John. *Mise-en-scène: Film Style and Interpretation*. New York: Wallflower, 2002.

Lazlo, Andrew. *Every Frame a Rembrandt: The Art and Practice of Cinematography*. Boston: Focal Press, 2000.

Mercado, Gustavo. *The Filmmaker's Eye: Learning and Breaking the Rules of Cinematic Composition*. Boston: Focal Press, 2011.

Winston, Brian. *Technologies of Seeing: Photography, Cinematography, and Television*. London: British Film Institute, 1996.

Camera Work

When you watch a film, you see it through the camera's eye, so where the camera is placed and how it moves are crucial constituents of film meaning.

Shots vary enormously in meaning. Close-ups often convey a sense of intimacy, but in this image, the close-up of the character from *The Conformist* actually conceals as much as it reveals. Elements of the image such as the averted eyes and the slash of the windscreen wiper across the face suggest duality of motive. He is in fact a fairly shady person who is launched on a mission of betrayal.

FIGURE 2.1 *The Conformist*. A close-up of this character is suggestive of his immorality.

Usually, in a medium shot, one can see the bodies of the characters, and one can also see much more of the setting in which the action occurs than in a close-up, which tends to eliminate setting entirely from view. In a medium shot the emphasis is usually on the interaction between the characters, not on the relation between character and environment. This image from *The Philadelphia Story*, for example, portrays a struggle between people; the film is constructed primarily from close-ups and medium shots and is very little concerned with the

FIGURE 2.2 *The Philadelphia Story.* A classic medium shot.

social and physical environment in which the social and personal problems at the center of the story play out.

Long shots tend toward impersonality and objectivity. Much more of the social or physical environment is included within the visual frame. In this image from *Bicycle Thieves*, director Vittorio De Sica has placed the camera at a distance from his primary character, a poor man living in government subsidized housing in the impoverished Italy of the post-World War II era who has just heard he finally has been given a job. Notice in this image that the long shot has the effect of making the character seem small in comparison to his physical environment. The discrepancy in size foreshadows the frustration of his yearnings; the world will indeed prove too big for him.

FIGURE 2.3 *Bicycle Thieves.* This long shot captures the sense that the economic environment is more powerful than the main character.

In the following examples from *On the Waterfront,* we see how the three different kinds of shots are used at different moments in the same film to portray an evolving relationship between two characters. The film concerns a dockworker, Terry Molloy, who is involved with a corrupt union. He aids them in killing a fellow dockworker, Joey Doyle, who has decided to testify against corruption to federal investigators. As the story evolves, Terry falls in love with Joey's sister, Edie, and he comes under the influence of a reforming priest. Eventually, he decides to testify against the corrupt union.

In the medium shot, Terry and Edie renew their acquaintance and try to get to know more about each other. As their relationship grows in importance and intimacy, Terry will move away from the male group he belongs to at the beginning of the film. The medium shot allows both of them to be in the frame at the same time and implicitly establishes a relationship (or the possibility of a relationship) between them.

As their relationship deepens during the course of the film, the interactions between Terry and Edie are characterized by an increasing use of close-ups. As the emotional distance between them lessens, the distance of the camera to their faces in the compositions also lessens. In a small but significant compositional move, in a scene in which the two characters debate contending moral positions, the director Elia Kazan places Terry slightly lower than Edie in the alternating close-ups, since his moral or philosophical position—that life is a struggle and one must hit first before one is hit—is portrayed as inferior to that of Edie, who argues that people should care for one another.

FIGURES 2.4 – 2.6 *On the Waterfront*. A close-up, a long shot, and a medium shot depict moments in an evolving romantic relationship.

Finally, the long shot depicts a moment when Terry confesses to Edie his role in the murder of her brother. Notice how the composition emphasizes the environment, which has had such a negative effect on both of their lives.

Film directors often alternate long and close shots in the same sequence for semantic ends. In a famous sequence from Alfred Hitchcock's *The Birds*, Melanie Daniels delivers two lovebirds to the home of a man she is pursuing, Mitch Brenner. Melanie is a "playgirl," an independent young woman of a kind which in the early 1960s was frowned upon by Roman Catholic social conservatives like Hitchcock. She is not following what Hitchcock felt was an

FIGURES 2.7 & 2.8 *The Birds*. A close-up makes Melanie seem in charge, but a contrasting long shot in the same sequence suggests she is not. Nature is more powerful than she is.

appropriate "natural" role for women, and nature takes its revenge on her. The birds are a metaphor for the force in nature that makes us adhere to certain prescribed gender types and formulas. They evoke the idea of a Biblical plague sent to punish a wayward humanity.

In this sequence, Melanie actively breaks from the passive role women were assigned in romantic matters at the time the movie was made. She, not the man, undertakes "the chase." She rents a boat, crosses a bay alone, and drops off the birds at Mitch's house. In Hitchcock's vision of the world, this reversal of the traditional paradigm of male pursuer–female pursued constitutes a breach of the natural order, and that infraction of nature's rules should be punished. As she returns to the dock, mincing in a flirtatious way at Mitch, who waits on the dock, Melanie is attacked by a bird and wounded. The birds then proceed to devastate the town and kill people.

Hitchcock alternates shots during the bird delivery sequence to portray Melanie as someone who does not quite realize what she is getting into by disturbing the natural order of things and assuming a traditional male role of active sexual pursuit. A medium close shot of Melanie is used when she seems most in control of the situation, but long shots of the landscape make Melanie's boat look very small and very vulnerable. There is something ominous about how fragile the boat seems within the space of land and water. Once nature makes its power felt, Melanie will be pecked into a near comatose state, deprived of all power, and have to be carried away by Mitch in the end.

A camera can be situated at different levels in relation to the filmed action to create different meaning effects. Angle shots add emphasis to a point the film is making and resemble adverbs and adjectives in language in that they modify action and qualify characters. The meaning of an angle shot depends largely on context.

FIGURE 2.9 *Before the Devil Knows You're Dead.* A high angle suggests that someone who thought he was in control of a situation suddenly discovers that he is not.

The high angle shot can foster an impression of domination, as when someone looks down on someone else. But it can also be a way of suggesting that someone has lost power, stature, or moral value. In this image from *Before the Devil Knows You're Dead*, Andy learns that his plot to rob his parents' jewelry store has gone awry. Always in control, he suddenly finds himself at a loss. The high angle records this existential and emotional state.

Low angle shots, by looking up, often augment the size of characters and increase the visual mass of objects and people. The semantic effect is often to attribute superior power or authority or value to someone or something. In this example of a medium low angle shot from *The Searchers*, Ethan, the primary character, begins to demonstrate his superior knowledge of native tactics, a knowledge that places him above the other whites. His superiority to them is beginning to manifest itself, and John Ford therefore uses a low angle shot that also emphasizes how Ethan blends with the natural landscape around him.

FIGURE 2.10 *The Searchers*. A low angle shot suggests the superiority of one character.

The meaning of angle shots is not uniform, however. In the next low angle shot from *Mildred Pierce*, for example, the character is not meant to seem superior. He has just learned a friend has tried to frame him for murder, and he is trying to escape from the house in which the dead body lies. The low angle shot registers his feeling of entrapment.

All shots, including angle shots, can also be extreme, and the meanings generated are also usually extreme. In *The Birds*, Hitchcock uses extreme shots to depict Melanie Daniels as someone whose vulnerability ultimately will make her need male protection. In keeping with the theme of a Biblical plague sent to punish a misguided humanity, Hitchcock seems at times to evoke a sense of divine retribution in extreme high angle shots.

FIGURE 2.11 *Mildred Pierce*. A low angle shot used to suggest treachery and entrapment.

FIGURE 2.12 *The Birds*. Hitchcock uses extreme angles and shots to make his female character seem vulnerable.

Camera movement is another way of constructing a story and making meaning. Movement adds inflection and valuation to events or characters. It is a way for the director to intrude upon the action and to more forcefully situate or align the audience in certain ways.

The pan shot is often used to make connection. Often such connections can be for the purpose of establishing social relations or for making points about social groups. Jean Renoir's *Grand Illusion* (1937) is an anti-war film concerning French prisoners of war. Renoir was a humanist who believed in a fundamental humanity in everyone that transcends class, national, and ethnic differences. In this sequence from the film, he simultaneously moves the camera on a track and pans around a table in a prisoner-of-war camp in a way that connects the different men and implies equality amidst differences. Each comes from a different profession or class or ethnicity. The apparent seamlessness of the camera's circular motion suggests the deeper bond of connection between the men that is more important than their apparent differences of rank, class, or ethnicity.

Moving shots initially were one-directional track shots, but more recent technology (cameras on wheels, steadicams, hand-held cameras, drones) allows for a greater semantic diversity of moving shots. An example of a traditional straight tracking shot occurs in Stanley Kubrick's *Paths of Glory*. The film tells the story of World War I soldiers who are ordered to take an enemy position

FIGURES 2.13 – 2.16 *Grand Illusion.* A pan shot rotates clockwise from upper left to include everyone in a community of equals, despite their class differences.

FIGURES 2.17 & 2.18 *Paths of Glory*. In this anti-war film, several tracking shots are used to convey the futility of the combat.

and fail in a calamitous charge across no man's land. The charge across no man's land is done as a series of tracking shots whose images of carnage emphasize the impossibility and irrationality of the undertaking.

Modern dolly shots afford a much greater flexibility and range of movement. In this dolly shot from *Before the Devil Knows You're Dead*, Andy, the brother who has stolen from his company to support a more lavish lifestyle than he can afford, is finally about to be caught. His boss announces that the company will be audited by the Internal Revenue Service, and it is clear that the audit will surely expose Andy's theft. The sequence begins with the camera behind Andy. We see his colleagues, and the shot reinforces a sense that he belongs to a work community to which he has responsibilities. That his back is to the

FIGURES 2.19 – 2.22 *Before the Devil Knows You're Dead*. A dolly shot acts to separate an unethical character from his community of coworkers as his malfeasance begins to come to light.

camera is not a good sign. Andy seems to have something to hide, as indeed he does. The camera begins to dolly in, pushing toward Andy. It passes him and swings around to face him. The effect of the dolly shot is to separate him from his community of coworkers. By the end of the shot, he is isolated in the frame, alone in his guilt and his irresponsibility. The camera movement both renders the dramatic situation and acts as a judgment against him.

A mobile camera augments meaning in *The Shining* (1980). The camera follows a young boy, Danny, as he tricycles through a hotel resort his father is

FIGURE 2.23 *The Shining.* As it follows Danny through the corridors of the hotel, the camera emphasizes motifs that suggest the role of repetition and circularity in human life.

looking after for the winter. The film concerns a conflict between human civilization and the natural impulses that underlie it.

Many visual elements of the film emphasize the distinction between mind and body, between our ability to use our cognitive abilities to build cooperative communities through communication on the one hand and our natural, physical, animal impulses that lead us to harm one another for the sake of individual survival on the other. Danny's circular movements through the hotel corridors reinforce the idea that time is in some sense circular. The present repeats the past because our natural instinctual urges, to survive and to reproduce by obtaining food and sex, reappear—endlessly—in human life. We are haunted by them, much as Jack is haunted by the ghosts of the hotel. Danny's circles are a good metaphor for this aspect of human life because any point in a circular movement is at the same time both new and a repetition. Movement forward only repeats what came before. In the hotel, the past inhabits the present, much as our primitive physical urges repeat endlessly and never go away. This is why the ghosts from the past are linked to the kitchen and bathrooms, to our repetitive natural processes of eating and excretion. Danny's apparently manic tricycle rising nicely embodies this sense of human time in nature.

Lenses can also be used to communicate ideas. In *Road to Perdition* (2002), for example, the son of a powerful gangster acts irresponsibly and betrays his father's interests. He ultimately will be sacrificed because he is such a liability. In this sequence, he sits at a table while his father walks past him, moving away. Rather than stay focused on the son, the camera remains focused on the father, and, as he moves further away, the son falls out of focus. The blurred image is held for a few beats. The fact that the son is in the foreground draws attention to the absence of focus. It is as if the audience were being alerted both to his demotion within the gangster community and to his ultimate fate.

FIGURE 2.24 *The Road to Perdition.* Loss of focus is used on a character who is about to lose stature and, eventually, his life.

Movements of the focal length (zooms) can also create meaning effects. In the following sequence from *The Godfather* (1972), Michael Corleone offers to kill two enemies of his mafia family. In the film, the old Don is almost killed and one of his sons is gunned down. Michael is obliged to take up the mantle of gang leader to save the family. He kills the two enemies, flees to Sicily, and returns in time to kill off the rest of the family's enemies. A conservative film, *The Godfather* argues in favor of strong patriarchal leadership.

FIGURES 2.25 – 2.28 *The Godfather*. In this sequence of images, the camera zooms in on the new godfather of the mafia family, endowing him with visual authority at the very moment he lays claim to authority within the clan.

The sequence begins with controversy between Michael's brother and the family lawyer. Dressed alike, neither is individuated, and neither has a clear sense of what to do. A singular authority lodged in a courageous individual is missing, the film suggests; democracy and discussion are only making a bad situation worse. The lawyer leans over the new don who does not possess enough authority to enforce his decisions. After a pause, Michael, seated in the middle of the room, begins to speak and outline a plan. As he does so, the camera slowly zooms in towards him. When it reaches a medium close-up, he announces in conclusion that he will kill the two adversaries. The zoom-in contrasts with the back-and-forth panning movement that characterized the hectic argument between the lawyer and Michael's brother. It offers a sense of visual singularity that correlates with Michael's singular, decisive, and authoritative announcement of a solution to the family's problems. By slowly zooming in on Michael, the camera separates him visually from everyone else and insinuates that he, not they and their indecisive discussion, will lead the way. What is needed, the film asserts in a very conservative vein, is a strong individual leader, not discussion and democracy.

Quite different effects arise from the zoom out. Unlike the zoom in, which has the effect of focusing attention on an object or a person, the zoom out moves away from things, diminishes them in size, and draws in comparatively more surrounding space. In this example from *Klute* (1971), a young woman receives a harassing phone call from a serial killer, hangs up and, as the camera draws away from her in the zoom out, looks smaller and smaller in the frame as the room around her grows bigger and bigger. Her loneliness and vulnerability are underscored by this visual strategy. The film argues that her single lifestyle is dangerous and depicts her finding safety and protection in a traditional marriage.

Hitchcock combines a zoom and a dolly shot in *The Birds* to portray a return to order in the Brenner household. Initially Mitch, the son, is made to appear dominated and infantilized by his mother. He is referred to as a "kid," and he wears what at the time would have been seen as an "effeminate" apron as he helps her with domestic labor. When nature strikes in the form of bird attacks, the woman becomes helpless and hysterical, and he manifests a cool capability that appears to "masculinize" him. If the mother dominated the family initially, after several bird attacks a new family (and social) order appears in which, both visually and personally, Mitch dominates. Hitchcock, after the final bird attack on the house, dollies and zooms out, away from the mother, until she is small in the back of the frame and Mitch is large and dominant in the foreground. The film affirms the "natural" gender order .

Cinematographers often use different kinds of lenses to create different visual and semantic effects. Lenses can vary in focal length, and these differences can be exploited by cinematographers or directors to create images that vary from crisp and well-defined to unclear and smudgy, sometimes within the same film. Edward Dmytryk very deliberately set out to use the varying possibilities

FIGURES 2.29 – 2.31 *Klute*. A zoom out depicts a woman in a dangerous environment.

FIGURE 2.32 – 2.34 *The Birds*. Hitchcock uses a combined zoom and dolly shot to portray a new gender order in the Brenner family.

of different lenses to construct an important visual motif in his film *Crossfire* (1947). A murderer is initially presented as being innocent, and Dmytryk wished the audience to see him in a manner that would suggest clarity and transparency of character, as if everything he said were true because one could see so clearly what he feels and thinks.

Notice how clear and well-defined the character's face is in the first image. The 50mm lens used in this shot creates the impression that he is as virtuous as he claims to be. In the second image, from later in the film, the same character is shot using a 35mm lens, one that creates a less crisp or well-defined image. By this point, the man's motives are in doubt; we have seen him commit another murder, and we now know that we were mistaken in our earlier judgment of him. The less crisp image removes him from the visual realm of transparent innocence and virtuous clarity. Near the end of the film, when the murderer is about to be trapped by the police, Dmytryk switches to a 25mm lens. The character's face is now smudgy and almost out of focus. Dmytryk wished to suggest that the murderer's true character, with its potential for prejudice and brutality, is now becoming visible. As the film has evolved, his appearance of virtue has been eroded to reveal nasty prejudices and brutal urges.

FIGURES 2.35 – 2.37 *Crossfire*. As a character evolves through the course of a film about a murder, he is pictured with three different lenses of differing degrees of resolution.

Deep focus photography permits objects in the back of the frame as well as the front to remain in focus at the same time. In the following example of deep focus photography from *The Best Years of Our Lives*, two army veterans are pictured as equals even though they come from different class backgrounds. One of them, Al, the man standing in the foreground, has just told his old pal Fred, who is in the phone booth in the background, to leave his daughter alone. Fred is unhappily married and in love with Al's daughter, but he agrees to say goodbye to the young woman. While he telephones, Al watches. The image defines a rupture in their community of equals, but although Fred in the background is diminished by the conversation they have just had, a sense of equality and fairness of treatment is maintained because both men are in focus. The film is an argument in favor of the fair treatment of all veterans of World War II, despite their class background, and its visual style reinforces this argument by treating all characters with visual equality.

Filters placed over the camera lens can also add meaningful qualifiers to the action. In this image from *A History of Violence* (2005), a gangster's house is filmed using a red filter to suggest hellishness and a level of immorality that exceeds normal bounds. During the course of this sequence, the gangster will order his men to kill his own brother.

FIGURE 2.38 *The Best Years of Our Lives.* Deep focus photography.

FIGURE 2.39 *A History of Violence*. A red filter allows a man's house to appear to be infernal, as indeed it is.

Student Assignment: *The Birds* (1.35.00 to 1.37.00)

Do a shot-by-shot analysis of the sequence, paying special attention to the cinematography. This film argues that social order is best maintained by strong men. Gender inequality, it contends, is necessary in society. Women should be subordinate to men. Lydia, the mother, has dominated her household, and Mitch, her son, has been subordinate. How does that change in the course of this sequence? How does the camera work further the film's argument?

Student Assignment: *Before the Devil Knows You're Dead* (28:00 to 30:15)

Using the vocabulary from this chapter, describe the sequence. How is director Sidney Lumet using different kinds of shots to convey psychological and emotional states? How are the zoom in and the zoom out used to depict Andy's situation?

Student Assignment: *Masculin/Feminin* (1956) (30:00 to 33:18)

Describe the way the camera is used in this sequence. How is it different from camera use in typical Hollywood releases? Why might Godard choose to shoot in this way? For example, why have the cameraman follow Paul and Madeleine through the room when, arguably, it would have been easier to hold back and shoot the room from a single, positioned shot? Or why swing the camera around, separating Paul and Madeleine? Why do you think the camera follows him and not her? What might Godard accomplish through this decision?

FIGURES 2.40 & 2.41 *Masculin/Feminin*. Godard radically changes camera perspective in a way that departs from standard Hollywood usage.

FURTHER READING

Barclay, Steven. *The Motion Picture Image: From Film to Digital*. Boston: Focal Press, 2000.

Block, Bruce. *The Visual Story*. New York: Focal Press, 2008.

Brown, Blair. *Cinematography*. New York: Focal Press, 2012.

Eyman, Scott. *Five American Cinematographers*. Metuchen: Scarecrow, 1987.

Nilsen, Vladimir. *The Cinema as a Graphic Art*. New York: Hill & Wang, 1959.

Salt, Barry. *Film Style and Technology: History and Analysis*. London: Starwood, 1992.

Schaefer, Dennis, and Larry Salvato. *Masters of Light: Conversations with Contemporary Cinematographers*. Berkeley: University of California Press, 1984.

Thompson, Roy. *Grammar of the Shot*. Boston: Focal Press, 1988.

Editing

Editing is the art of selection and combination. An editor combines shots and images in ways that illuminate character, suggest ideas, or stage conflicts. The editor also combines scenes into a coherent and unified narrative. S/he maintains the continuity of the story.

Storytelling often depends on the linking of causes and consequences or motives and actions. A character behaves in one way, and that cause generates effects that appear in the next scene or image. In *Mildred Pierce*, for example, the main character, who is not yet divorced from her husband, sleeps with another man. The film cuts to her husband waiting to tell her that one of her daughters has caught pneumonia and is about to die. The cause–effect editing here serves a moral purpose. It is as if Mildred were being reprimanded for leading what, in the mid-1940s, was too independent a life.

FIGURES 3.1 & 3.2 In *Mildred Pierce*, the editing links events in a temporal logic but also in a moral logic.

Stanley Kubrick uses editing to portray his main character Jack Torrance as having a dark side that is not evident to the public in an early editing sequence in *The Shining*. During his interview with the manager of the Overlook Hotel, where Jack will work as caretaker, Jack appears to be a polite and civilized man.

FIGURES 3.3 – 3.5 *The Shining*. A dissolve edit emphasizes the continuity between a man's polite public persona and his violent private self.

But Kubrick juxtaposes this sequence with another, using a slow dissolve to emphasize the continuity between the public persona Jack offers the world and the private one he keeps at home. The dissolve edit takes us to Jack's apartment, where his wife Wendy tells a doctor about Jack's alcoholism and his physical abuse of their son. The editing deepens our sense of Jack's character and exposes a side that he keeps hidden from public view. It also sets the stage for the movie's larger theme—that humans are both human and animal at once.

Editing can also show characters in the course of transformation over time. In this famous sequence from *Blonde Venus* (1932), a woman's rise from

FIGURES 3.6 – 3.9 *Blonde Venus*. A montage editing sequence depicts transformation of character.

poverty to fame is depicted in a series of images that underscore both the magical quality of the transformation and her pluck in being able to pull it off. Her transformation is a token of powers that render ironic her conversion at the end of the film into a loyal, submissive housewife. The tweaking of the nose of patriarchy in the editing sequence is reinforced by her playfully lesbian flirting with one of the women in her dance troupe and by her ironically butch tuxedo.

The editor can also combine shots and images to stage conflicts. *Michael Clayton* concerns a conflict between a moral character and an immoral corporation. Michael is initially portrayed as someone who is willing to put aside moral scruples to do his job for his law firm. He cleans up messes created by wealthy clients of the firm. His friend Arthur takes a difference course: he discovers criminal wrongdoing, sets about exposing it, and is murdered. After first siding with the firm and the corporation against Arthur, Michael finally comes to his senses and sees that the heroic quest Arthur set out on is one that he himself must take up. He exposes the corruption.

In an early editing sequence, Michael is depicted doing his job. The sequence shows how corrupt his work is and simultaneously suggests that he might eventually be able to rise above the corruption. He has been assigned to help a wealthy client who struck a jogger with one of his numerous expensive sports cars and left the scene of the accident. Michael's role as janitor for his law firm requires a high tolerance for unethical behavior. As the sequence begins, he is portrayed as a tiny insignificant figure in comparison to the client's row of expensive cars. The image conveys the sense of his unimportance. He is a servant of the wealthy.

In the next image, he is blackened out and shot from behind, as befits his role as someone who puts aside his own moral scruples to help those without any. He erases his own identity and becomes an anonymous functionary performing unethical tasks for others. But as the sequence unfolds and as the client tries to avoid responsibility, the camera treats Michael more positively. The client is depicted moving around in an uncertain way, like a trapped animal trying to elude capture. Michael is in contrast a rock of stability and is shown in close-up, thinking about the situation. The close-up also functions to separate Michael visually from the client and his world. Michael appears to be on a visual island of his own. After cutting back to the client, moving around and complaining, the camera shoots up at Michael from a slight low angle, making him seem elevated above the corrupt situation he finds himself in and once again isolating him in the frame and separating him from the ambient darkness.

The sequence thus depicts Michael as someone who does an unsavory job well but who has, possibly, the potential in him for better. But notice how the sequence ends with an image of Michael's face awash in darkness. No matter how much good there may be within him, he is, at this point of the film, in a world unlit by any clear moral or ethical light.

When an editor puts parts of a movie together, s/he can use a number of principles to guide each edit such as similitude, parallel, contrast, irony, etc.

FIGURES 3.10 – 3.15 *Michael Clayton*. In this editing sequence, Michael does his job of janitor, cleaning up the legal messes of the wealthy, but the camera work and composition suggest he has the potential in him to be better.

For example, one of the simplest kinds of editing—the shot reverse shot editing sequence that depicts two characters interacting—lends itself to both similitude and contrast. The camera position changes from one character's point of view to the other, reversing the angle of vision so that the image alternates from one character's face to the other. It is a simple technique, but sometimes it is done in a way that layers in meaning. This shot reverse shot sequence from *Drive* (2011), for example, emphasizes the commonality between the two characters by locating them in complementary positions within the frame. The editing emphasizes the growing emotional relationship between the two by matching them in adjacent images.

FIGURES 3.16 & 3.17 *Drive*. Complementary composition emphasizes the harmonious relationship between the characters.

FIGURES 3.18 & 3.19 *Hyenas*. Continuity editing is used to make a connection between human actions and those of animals.

The linking of similar shots can be used to create parallels between things or metaphoric associations between actions and ideas. For example, in Djibril Diop Mambety's *Hyenas* (1992) a wealthy woman returns to her hometown and asks the villagers to kill an old enemy who is now the respected and well-liked mayor. She offers the villagers Western consumer goods such as televisions, and, in the end, they commit the murder for her. Mambety occasionally pauses in the storytelling to cut away to images of hyenas, just as the villagers are tormenting the mayor. He is equating the villagers' predatory actions with those of the hyenas.

Combining dissimilar shots can have a wide variety of functions, from highlighting thematic contrasts to emphasizing personal conflicts. *Thelma and Louise* (2001) concerns two women who are obliged to flee the law and their traditional feminine lives. As they move away from their old world, they take on more masculine traits, becoming more independent, capable, and strong. If

FIGURES 3.20 & 3.21 *Thelma and Louise*. Men, in this film of female escape from traditional roles, are portrayed in dark indoor settings while the escaping women are set in open landscapes.

the domestic world of the home was in the past associated with a more traditionally feminine role for women, the open road and the Wild West were often
linked to masculinity in the American cultural lexicon. As the women progress,
increasingly they take on the trappings of the Wild West and are associated with
cowboys, sunny open landscapes, and freedom of movement. The men who
chase them, in contrast, are posed in dark, often domestic settings where they
sit watching melodramas on television, condemned to live out the role assigned
to women in the past.

Juxtaposing dissimilar shots can also be used for a variety of rhetorical
ends. One is irony. Irony is created when images that contradict one another
are placed side by side. The makers of *Citizen Kane* wished to inspire a sense of
irony in the audience towards Kane. Kane runs for governor on a reform ticket
and pledges to prosecute corrupt political bosses like Jim Geddes. The first image
makes Kane appear to be larger than life. He looks like someone capable of
keeping his campaign promise.

But the image that follows conveys a very different sense of things. Kane
now looks diminutive. A man we soon learn is Jim Geddes looks down at him
and seems, visually, to have some kind of power over him. The meaning of
this new image is as yet unclear, but the editing alerts the viewer to think that
someone has power over Kane about which Kane is unaware, and it directs the
audience to feel that Kane's perceptions do not match reality. Indeed, it will
turn out that Geddes has information about Kane that will ruin his political
career.

Editing often serves a polemical or ideological purpose because it allows
filmmakers to shape the audience's perceptions by combining pieces of film into
sequences that determine how the audience sees a situation and the players in
it. *Apocalypse Now* (1979) depicts the Vietnam War, which lasted from the
mid-1950s to 1975, from a conservative perspective. During the war, the US
tried to prevent a national liberation movement, committed to the egalitarian
economic ideals of communism, from taking over the country. Debate raged in
the US between liberals, who opposed the war and felt it was unjustified, and

FIGURES 3.22 & 3.23 *Citizen Kane*. Kane shot from one angle appears to be triumphant, but, from another angle in an adjacent image, we see him as being in someone else's power.

conservatives, who felt greater force should be used to win decisively. Many civilian Vietnamese supported the liberation movement, and the US military was guilty of atrocities against the civilian population. In the most famous instance, at My Lai in 1968, several hundred women, children, and old people were murdered because their village men were away fighting the war against the American invaders. *Apocalypse Now* audaciously depicts such atrocities as justified.

In this action sequence, a squadron of US Air Cavalry attacks an enemy village. The sequence begins with the helicopters arriving. The sound of their arrival alerts the villagers, and a group of school children is shown fleeing to safety. But director Francis Ford Coppola makes sure the audience sees that, behind this façade of civilian life, the village conceals an arsenal of heavy weapons which come into play against the Americans. The Vietnamese are thereby coded as treacherous and duplicitous. They seem to be civilians, but in fact they are enemy soldiers in hiding. By portraying the Vietnamese as inter-changeably civilian or military, Coppola prepares the way for an argument justifying the killing of civilians.

As this sequence begins, an American soldier is wounded, and the film cuts away to the leader of the squadron, flying above in a helicopter, who voices concern for his men. He orders a helicopter to land and help the wounded. This codes the Americans as caring and good. A helicopter lands to evacuate the wounded soldier. But a woman runs back from the same direction the school children fled to. She flings a hat into the helicopter containing a bomb, and the helicopter blows up. As with the hidden weapons, the Vietnamese are coded as treacherous. The sequence cuts away again to the squadron leader who pronounces judgment on her action: "Fucking savages." A helicopter begins to chase the fleeing woman. In a voiceover, a soldier calls her an "assassin" and he asks his pilot to put the skid of the helicopter "up her ass." He then shoots her as she flees.

FIGURES 3.24 – 3.32 *Apocalypse Now*. In this editing sequence, director Francis Coppola and screenwriter John Milius argue that the Vietnamese adversaries of the US military during the Vietnam War used sneaky tactics, concealing military weapons in civilian settings. The film justifies atrocities against civilians.

Long editing sequences are often referred to as "montage" sequences. Early montage sequences such as those in *Battleship Potemkin* (1925) and *Intolerance* (1916) exploited the possibilities of selecting and combining shots for a range of effects, from suspense to indictment. Long montage sequences became less common as the movie industry consolidated. With the regimentation of production, there was less room for the creative and oftentimes political use of technique. The emergence of "art cinema" after World War II and in the 1960s revived an interest in earlier techniques such as montage. Noteworthy examples were the drug scenes in *Easy Rider* (1969) and *Midnight Cowboy* (1969), the sex scenes in *Zabriskie Point* (1970), and the death scene in *The Wild Bunch* (1969). Art gave way to commerce once again the 1970s and 1980s, but with the emergence of a new independent cinema since 1990, filmmakers have once again turned to non-realist techniques such as montage. Montage editing works to portray a character in *The Girl in the Cafe*. Lawrence, a boring government bureaucrat who lives a tedious and empty personal life until he meets Gina, a young woman who is much more spontaneous and politically radical than he, is introduced through a very long editing sequence that begins with one dominant sentiment and ends with a very different one. The sequence is about the possibility of personal transformation, and the transformation in the sequence itself as it unfolds is suggestive of personal plasticity and flexibility.

We first see Lawrence brushing his teeth to the left of the screen. A large dark block separates him from the right side of the screen which consists of his closet where we see his "role," the clothing that is his identity as a bureaucrat—neat white shirt, blue suit, red or blue tie. Lawrence is clearly a limited person, as the sliver he is assigned in the image suggests. But he is at odds with the role (the clothes) he has in life. There is a gap or separation between him and it, so the editing sequence begins by suggesting some hope for him by depicting the distance between him and his official role in life.

As the editing sequence progresses, we see him getting ready for work—breakfasting, walking down a corridor, carrying an umbrella—and then at work, where we see him being ignored by colleagues who pass a paper back and forth across him while he looks down reading. He walks down more long corridors in more highly symmetrical compositions. He seems to have no personality and no real contact with anyone. He is an anonymous blue figure without animation or vitality. He is uniform and he seems to wear a uniform. Everything in the images suggests a boring sameness and a sterile order. Lawrence, walking down the street, holding an umbrella to protect him from the rain, looks down and shuts his eyes. It is a moment of enormous despair and personal sorrow, as if his routine life were almost too much for him. But at the very end of the sequence, the camera switches from Lawrence to Gina. Gina also walks under an umbrella and holds her hand out to feel the rainfall. The editing sequence connects the two characters, and it suggests that, with her help, there is a chance that Lawrence might also be able to experience life firsthand. It is a subtle visual cue that alerts us to the fact that he might benefit if he happens upon someone like Gina—as indeed he does.

FIGURES 3.33 – 3.38 *The Girl in the Cafe.* A character is portrayed in this long editing sequence as a boring bureaucrat for whom there is still some hope.

Student Assignment: *Michael Clayton* (26.24 to 27.12)

Do a shot-by-shot analysis of the sequence. How are Barry and the other men in the office portrayed visually? When Michael enters, what is most striking about the image? In the next shot, the camera looks over his shoulder and down at Barry and the other men. What might this be insinuating about Michael's difference from them? Finally, Michael walks between two significant objects in the next shot—an airplane hangar that looms over him and an open sun-lit landscape. What is the significance of the image and of the voice-over for him and for the moral choices he must make during the course of the film?

Student Assignment: *Alien* (1979) (32:29 to 34:29)

Using language from this chapter, describe the editing in this sequence. By contemporary horror standards, the editing in *Alien* might be considered slow; describe the sense of time and space in this sequence. Are we given a sense of peace and tranquillity, or suspense? How is that sense conveyed to the viewer? How does this sequence prepare us for the narrative development of this section of the film? How does this sequence move the film forward?

Student Assignment: *The Man with the Movie Camera* (1929)
(14:55 to 17:00)

Like *Battleship Potemkin*, *The Man with the Movie Camera* is an example of Russian montage filmmaking. Describe the juxtapositions of images in this sequence. What emotions do you think Dziga Vertov is trying to evoke in his audience? Which juxtapositions suggest which reactions? While the sequence isn't narrative in the traditional sense of the term, do you think that it tells a story? Why, or why not?

FURTHER READING

Dmytryk, Edward. *On Film Editing: An Introduction to the Art of Film Construction.* Boston/London: Focal Press, 1984.

Eisenstein, Sergei. *Film Form.* New York: Harcourt, Brace, Jovanovich, 1949.

Fairservice, Don. *Film Editing: History, Theory, and Practice. Looking at the Invisible.* New York: Palgrave, 2001.

Murch, Walter. *In the Blink of an Eye: A Perspective on Film Editing.* Los Angeles: Silman-James Press, 2001.

Opel, Valerie. *Film Editing: The Art of the Expressive.* New York: Wallflower, 2003.

Reisz, Karel. *The Technique of Film Editing.* Boston: Elsevier/Focal Press, 2010.

Art Direction

Art direction or production design constructs the visual and aural environment of a film. The choice of location or the design of the set is an active agent in creating meaning, as are lighting, color, and sound.

Location and set design are capable of an enormous variety of visual and semantic effects. Sets are often constructed with thematic ends in mind.

The set of *The Shining* contains numerous Native American motifs that remind the audience that the Overlook Hotel was built on a Native American burial ground. The hotel is a metaphor for America and for the way it "overlooks" its history of genocide against Native Americans. The motifs are evocative of this important theme of the movie.

FIGURE 4.1 *The Shining*. Native American motifs on the walls and floors of the hotel connect with one of the movie's themes.

Natural settings can be used in a variety of ways to create meaning. John Ford filmed *The Searchers* in Monument Valley, Utah, and he draws on the discrepancy between the rock monuments and the humans to map out a significant transformation that occurs during the course of the film. Nature initially seems more powerful than human civilization, and that idea is rendered in images in which the rock outcroppings loom over the men as they pursue a band of Native Americans who have stolen cattle. But, as the film progresses, the men are depicted riding up slopes and attaining higher positions in relation to the landscape. And by the end, when settler civilization triumphs, the main character stands on top of one of the outcroppings and surveys the valley (and the Native Americans) below. The danger posed by nature (and by wild human behavior at odds with the norms of white civilization for which the Native Americans serve as a metaphor) has been overcome.

FIGURES 4.2 & 4.3 *The Searchers*. The natural landscape is used to create meaning in this western.

Sets are not only background for the action of the film. Filmmakers often draw on set elements to make meaning or to reinforce a point being made in the action. For example, when these two characters in *The Philadelphia Story* argue, a line from the window stands between them, reinforcing the sense of conflict.

FIGURE 4.4 *The Philadelphia Story*. A visual detail in the set—the vertical line between the characters—helps to portray their conflict.

Similarly, in *The Shining*, the fact that a character is poised between civilized life, with all of its norms and rules regarding polite behavior, and animal life, with all of its predatory violence and incivility, is suggested by a line in the set. Notice in this image that Jack sits in front of a line that divides his head in two, suggesting the conflict in the movie between the civil and animal realms, a conflict that is played out through his character.

The sets of *Blade Runner* (1982) reinforce its theme of dehumanization. People metaphorically become machines for large corporations that

FIGURE 4.5 *The Shining*. Lines in the set are used to reinforce the idea of a conflict between civility and animality in human life.

provide ample rewards for a few while condemning the majority to lives of drudgery and slavery. The production designers convey this idea through set elements that loom over characters and make them seem small and insignificant.

FIGURES 4.6 & 4.7 *Blade Runner.* Set elements dominate characters visually to suggest how the Tyrell Corporation dominates their lives.

Specific set locations such as bedrooms, bathrooms, and kitchens can also be made to resonate with meaning. In *The Shining*, for example, a division between the mind and the body, the realm of civil communication and the realm of involuntary physical urges, is suggested by the recurring use of bathrooms. Civility is associated with "shining," a mental power that allows people to communicate without words. Civility makes us human rather than animal, and "shining" is a metaphor for those aspects of civility such as care and empathy for others that allow humans to rise above their animal natures and to become civilized humans in cooperative communities. While Wendy and her son Danny remain in the realm of civility, Jack, the father, loses his mind and succumbs to animalistic natural impulses. He indulges his appetites for drink and sex, and he becomes increasingly abusive in language and action. He first breaks the rules of civil speech, then the rules of civil behavior. In the end, he tries to murder his family.

FIGURE 4.8 *The Shining*. A bathroom is an important metaphor for the conflict between mind and body.

In the film's set design, light across the top of the screen is consistently associated with "shining," the ability to see into the nature of things and to communicate without words with others. Shining is linked to civility and to the bonds that create human communities. It is juxtaposed to uncontrolled rage and the animal ability to do violence to others. In this image a boy stands looking into a mirror and "shining." The light at the top of the frame and the toilet at the bottom suggest the conflict between mind and body at the heart of the film. The bodily realm of uncontrolled physical urges, a natural world of instinctive animal impulses that is kept in check by human civility, stands opposed to shining in the film's thematic structure.

Props and costumes should also be considered part of the meaning-making repertoire of art directors and production designers. In this sequence from *The Buccaneers* (1995), an independent woman talks to an English aristocrat with whom she is having an affair. He is a conservative traditionalist, she more modern and liberal in her sensibility. His attitudes toward women are strict and old-school, hers more sympathetic and feminist. Notice the props behind each of them. His is a bust that looks like it embodies the patriarchal tradition of ruling men, hers is a female figure who seems more whole and, in consequence, more human.

FIGURES 4.9 & 4.10 *The Buccaneers*. Props are used to comment on characters in this exchange between a conservative man and a liberal woman regarding social mores.

Furniture, mirrors, clocks, and statuettes from Malta can also play a role in augmenting meaning. For example, in this image from *The Conformist*, a film about Fascist Italy in the 1930s, a man who wishes to prove he is a good Fascist talks with a member of the party. To the side, featured quite prominently, is a piece of furniture that imitates Fascist architectural and interior design motifs, which favored rigidly straight lines suggesting the sense of order that Fascism supposedly brought to the world.

FIGURE 4.11 *The Conformist*. Furniture adds an element of meaning in this film about Italian Fascism.

FIGURE 4.12 *The Shining*. A costume evokes the Faust legend in which a man sells his soul to the devil.

Costume is often an element of meaning. One theme of *The Shining* is the violence done to Native Americans in the formation of America. At one point, Wendy Torrance wears a jacket with Native motifs on it that mirror the Native motifs on the floors and walls of the Overlook Hotel. Stanley Kubrick uses both set and costume to establish a sense of commonality between the victims of the violence perpetrated by the wealthy and the powerful in the establishing of America nationhood.

Changes in costume can also be ways of recording changes in a character. In *Laurel Canyon* (2002), Alex, a fairly conservative young woman, visits the home

FIGURES 4.13 & 4.14 *Laurel Canyon*. Alex, having worn tight, professional looking running gear before, now dons a hip t-shirt at a moment in the film when her character begins to change.

of her boyfriend's very hip mother. Alex becomes transformed by the experience, and her transformation is registered in a change in running clothes from severe and professional to loose and relaxed. After a hesitant start, she eventually puts on one of the mother's "AC/DC" t-shirts as part of her jogging gear. It suggests a new more flexible attitude.

Lighting varies across a spectrum from three-point lighting, which creates a shadowless effect, to back lighting, which produces a blacked out image. This image from *The Philadelphia Story* uses three-point lighting from three different sources to create a glowing appearance that is common to classical realism. It portrays a world without moral ambiguity or dangerous deception where the most one has to worry about is a little bad press from the gossip columns. The lighting normalizes the world depicted and makes it appear virtuous. As one would expect, the film is a comedy of manners rather than a moral tragedy or a social problem film.

FIGURE 4.15 *The Philadelphia Story.* Three-point lighting creates the appearance of a "normal" world.

At the other extreme from the sunny, well-lit world of *The Philadelphia Story* is the dark, menacing world of film noir. The genre earned its name from images in which characters are almost completely blacked out. The use of back lighting is appropriate to a story of duplicity, treachery, and betrayal in which motives are concealed and in which behavior that blurs moral boundaries is common. In the image from *Klute*, a film noir about prostitution and murder,

FIGURE 4.16 *Klute*. A modern film noir uses low key and backlit lighting to convey a sense of an immoral world.

notice how back lighting (placing the light source behind the figure rather than in front or to the side) works to create a sense of immersion in a world of dubious morality, in which one can lose one's identity, not to mention one's life, quickly.

Once again, however, one should not assume that the same visual device or effect always has the same meaning. Dark images are not always emblems of evil or signs of danger. They can also be used to create emotional effects, as in this image from *2046* that depicts a man who has chosen to give up the love of a young prostitute. She is in despair as he leaves, but one senses from this image that his emotional state is far from ebullient.

Light can also be hard or soft (using a diffusion filter). The image from *Chinatown* (1974) is characterized by hard key lighting at a 45-degree angle from the audience's right and a classic 45-degree height. Notice how it highlights outlines and adds a sense of clarity. In this film, such clarity is misleading (and the detective who is the main character is misled by it). Noah Cross only appears to be a virtuous member of the community; in truth, he

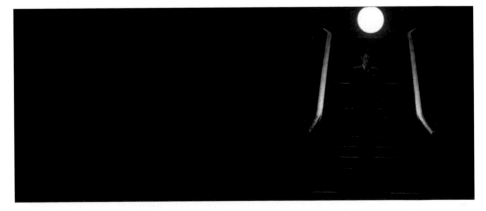

FIGURE 4.17 *2046*. A black image suggests an emotional state rather than a moral condition.

is corrupt and immoral. The perfect clarity of this image of him gets at those dimensions of his character by recording perfectly his appearance of respectability. Because the color balance of the image is also warm, the revelation of his perfidy becomes all the more shocking when contrasted with this mode of visual representation.

FIGURE 4.18 *Chinatown*. Hard lighting produces an appearance of clarity of character.

Diffused lighting produces a soft lighting effect in *Road to Perdition*, where gangster John Rooney is quite open about the criminal existence he leads. The light comes from a 90-degree angle relative to the view of the camera, and the key lighting is at head height in order to hit the actor's face below the hat brim. Notice how the color balance of the image adds a bluish, almost cadaverous tone to his skin. The diffuse lighting creates a soft, cool feel that subliminally communicates the sense of menace in this character.

FIGURE 4.19 *The Road to Perdition*. Diffuse lighting reinforces a sense of menace.

Some filmmakers have sought to use color to create dramatic, emotional, and semantic effects. Production designers often use the color of the background set to reinforce meanings. In this image from *Shame* (2011), for example, a man who is a sociopathic sex addict is depicted buying sex from a prostitute. His world is cold, alienated, and lacking in warm personal ties or emotional commitments. He preys regularly and repeatedly on women, when he is not buying sex, and he avoids establishing emotional bonds with them. Notice how the set suggests emotional vacancy as well as flatness of tone. It could be a hospital ward or a mental institution, and in part that is the point. Brandon is sick, and all the colors and compositions associated with him suggest coolness of affect, dissociation, and distance.

FIGURE 4.20 *Shame.* The coldness of the set is emblematic of the coldness of the main character's emotional life.

FIGURE 4.21 *Written on the Wind.* Color serves as a qualifier of character in this melodrama from the 1950s.

There is no single meaning to any one color motif across all films. Red, for example, can for obvious reasons be linked to violence, but it can also suggest powerful feelings or passions. In *Written on the Wind* (1956), Marylee, the spoiled daughter of a wealthy father, is associated with sexually passionate reds, while Mitch, the virtuous family friend from a humbler background, is portrayed in more natural-seeming greens and browns.

In contrast, red in *The Shining* is linked to dangerously uncontrolled rage. It is associated with aspects of nature that threaten to overwhelm the civil restraints that make us human. The set is characterized by elements that evoke the thematic conflict between civility and animality, the mind and the body, in human life. Colors are an important way of distinguishing these two realms. The color blue is linked to civility, self-control, empathy, and our human ability to communicate and to form cooperative communities. It is found on characters such as Halloran, Wendy, and her son, Danny, who care for others. Red, in contrast, is linked to violence, rage, and the animal-like behavior that results when civil restraint breaks down and the imperatives of individual survival take over. In the film, the characters that are most civil wear blue over red. In contrast, when Jack first loses control and has a violent dream of killing Wendy and Danny, he switches to wearing red over blue. It is a simple visual metaphor for his descent from civility into natural animality, from self-control to violent rage. When he finally leaves civility behind altogether and agrees to murder his family, it is, appropriately, in a very red bathroom.

FIGURE 4.22 – 4.24 *The Shining.* Colors are used in this movie to suggest the characters' varying placement in relation to the theme of civility and animality.

The saturation level of images can also be used for semantic effects. Saturated images have strong hues. Melodramas of the 1950s such as *Written on the Wind* use heavily saturated images to portray worlds charged with powerful emotions and eruptive passions.

FIGURE 4.25 *Written on the Wind*. Saturated color draws attention to these significant objects that are suggestive of sexuality.

In contrast, a film about human evil such as *Se7en* (1995) relics on desaturation to create images painted in a more somber tone appropriate to its theme. In this film world, heroism does not consist of grand gestures carried out in bright colors; it consists rather of a more dogged sense of persistence that produces unclear results.

Films are meant as much to be heard as to be seen, although the primacy of the visual experience often makes us forget that we are hearing sounds that are essential for conveying information, constructing characters, producing emotional effects, and creating meaning.

FIGURE 4.26 *Se7en*. A desaturated image portrays a world in which heroism also is toned down.

Movie music is designed to evoke reactions in audiences appropriate to the events depicted. *The Best Years of Our Lives* is a good example of the use of nondiegetic accompanying music (that is, music whose source is not found within the world of the story, or diegesis). When you watch it, you will notice how a particular musical motif or ostinato recurs at significant dramatic moments in a film that otherwise relies on very little music. The story is a melodrama, a tale of emotional and psychological struggle and healing, and the orchestral accompaniment more or less instructs the audience to respond in appropriately empathetic ways when the characters undergo an emotional trauma or achieve some kind of healing. The music in effect forces the audience to adopt the ideological argument of the film—that we should "feel" for the suffering of others, put aside selfish feelings or bottom-line business-as-usual mandates, and help them. By imposing an emotional reaction that might be characterized as sentimental, the film's sound designers get us to identify with others by empathizing with them.

Non-musical sound is a crucial element of meaning in film. In *The Shining*, a heart beats loudly at certain moments, and a coyote calls in the wild. These motifs suggest a world of fragile civility perched atop a much more powerful nature of violent urges that threaten it. The human mind, with its power to

FIGURE 4.27 *The Best Years of Our Lives*. A father is overcome with emotion as the music surges. He has just read a letter commending his son for bravery during World War II.

create civil communities through communication with others, is anchored in a body controlled by drives and instincts. When they erupt, they distort human speech. As blood pours from elevators, the voices of the characters suddenly sound as if they are under water.

FIGURE 4.28 *The Shining.* As blood pours from elevators, the voices of characters sound as if they are under water to suggest how animality overwhelms civility.

Spoken words are essential to meaning in film. Most spoken dialogue is informational. But speech is also a form of action, a means of getting attention, inflicting harm, gaining power, inciting emotion, etc. It is as much a part of the action of the film as the physical events. This is why actors often devote so much time and energy to learning how to deliver lines properly. One of the most famous schools of acting, Method acting, consists of finding in oneself memories and emotions that allow one to connect with the part and the words one is speaking more authentically, as if one's own feelings were being spoken. *On the Waterfront* is famous for its Method sequences, especially the one in the back of a car between Rod Steiger and Marlon Brando, the most famous of the Method actors. "I could have been a contender," Brando as Terry Molloy, the failed boxer, says, "instead of a bum, which is what I am." In this instance, emotional intensity and psychological authenticity are as much the result of Brando's famously moving delivery as it is of the twisted, non-grammatical sentences, which seem more "true" to the speech of the uneducated character he plays.

Two very skilled modern actors, Marisa Tomei and Philip Seymour Hoffman, use tone of voice and inflection in *Before the Devil Knows You're Dead* to depict character and to make plain the emotional problems that exist between characters. Tomei plays Gina, a gold-digger who has latched onto Andy, the Hoffman character. To keep her happy, he steals from his company

FIGURE 4.29 *On the Waterfront.* The Method technique of acting is used to evoke pathos and empathy.

and concocts a scheme to rob his parents' jewelry store. Tomei plays the character of Gina as whiney and spoiled, brassy and unempathetic. Her voice is sometimes tough, sometimes girly, and Tomei portrays her as someone who gets by with help from men but has little going for herself apart from her sexuality. Andy is an emotional mess whose relationship with his father bears residues of childhood trauma and disappointment. Little is said to describe what those traumas might have been, but Hoffman uses a flat-toned voice to communicate their deadly effect on his character's psychology. Andy has been rendered mildly sociopathic by whatever happened between him and his father in childhood, and sociopaths often lack an ability to empathize or to express emotion. That lack of human warmth is communicated in one exchange with his father. The father says, "I'm sorry I wasn't a better father," and Andy replies: "I'm sorry I wasn't a better son." The father speaks with real emotion, a real sense of pain, but Andy sounds like a robot speaking a memorized line that has no emotion whatsoever in it.

FIGURE 4.30 *Before the Devil Knows You're Dead*. Marisa Tomei portrays Gina as a ditzy, selfish, overly dependent gold-digger.

FIGURE 4.31 *Before the Devil Knows You're Dead*. Andy and his father trade lines, but the father speaks with emotion, while Philip Seymour Hoffman's delivery is flat-toned and without emotion.

Speech can also be a form of violence. It acts on people, destroying their happiness or sense of self worth. If Gina whines and Terry laments, Jack Torrance in *The Shining* curses, denounces, and taunts his wife Wendy. Civility in the film takes the form of verbal interactions that demonstrate respect and care for others, and the first sign that Jack has slipped out of civility and into animality occurs as he swears at Wendy when she interrupts his manic work and tells her to "get the fuck out of here." His verbal behavior is in striking contrast to her polite speech. Later, when he first tries to kill her, he taunts her and mimics her speech, using mockery as a form of violence.

FIGURE 4.32 *The Shining.* Verbal violence breaches civility and exposes the animality lying beneath.

Finally, silence has been used in a number of films as a way of making meaning. Usually, such silence occurs where it is supposed not to be, as in this sequence from *Road to Perdition* in which Michael Sullivan takes revenge on his former employer, John Rooney. From a distance, he fires a machine gun that we can only see as a bright muzzle flare surrounded by darkness. Rooney's bodyguards fall one by one until only he is left standing with his back turned to the killer. The falling rain adds a metaphoric dimension to an already highly symbolic moment, as if the killing constituted a visiting of retribution—a "hard rain"—on evildoers. That Michael does not appear until the end of the sequence makes his action seem like an act of divine justice.

FIGURE 4.33 – 4.35 *The Road to Perdition*. A sequence that would usually be shot with sound—the killing of men using a machine gun—is shot in silence, thus giving it a very different meaning.

Student Assignment: *The Shining* (1.43.30 to 1.49.18)

Do a shot-by-shot analysis of the sequence. It begins with Wendy's discovery that Jack has gone mad. Jack's writing suggests he has stepped outside civility. What other elements of art direction suggest this theme?

Student Assignment: *The Cabinet of Dr. Caligari* (1920) (5:14 to 7:16)

Describe the art direction of this sequence using the language that you've learned in this chapter. This film is considered to be an exemplar of German Expressionist film, an early genre that had particular influence on the film noir style of the mid-twentieth century. Consider some of the films noirs that you've seen—what elements of film noir do you see in *Caligari*? What do you think director Robert Wiene is attempting to accomplish with his art direction?

FIGURE 4.36 *The Cabinet of Dr. Caligari.* The set characterizes the world in this celebrated example of German Expressionism.

FURTHER READING

Affron, Charles. *Sets in Motion: Art Direction and Film Narrative.* New Brunswick: Rutgers University Press, 1995.

Alton, John. *Painting With Light.* New York: Macmillan, 1949.

Barnwell, Jane. *Production Design: Architects of the Screen.* New York: Wallflower, 2004.

Birtwistle, Andy. *Cinesonica: Sounding Film and Video.* New York: Palgrave Macmillan, 2010.

Ettedqui, Peter. *Production Design and Art Direction.* Woburn: Focal, 1999.

LoBrutto, Vincent. *By Design: Interviews with Film Production Designers.* Westport: Praeger, 1992.

Sylbert, Paul. *Final Cut: The Making and Breaking of Film.* New York: Seabury, 1974.

Tashiro, C. S. *Pretty Pictures: Production Design and the History of Film.* Austin: University of Texas Press, 1998.

The Art of Film. New York: Films Media Group, 2006.

Narration

When you see a movie, it is easy to ignore the fact that you are being told a story in a particular way. The term for the way a story is told is narration.

How is narration different from the story the film is about? Imagine seeing the events that a movie is about in their entirety—every single second of them. A movie that covers six days would take six days to see. You would see events, but you would not really see a narrative, a "told story."

A narrative tells a story by selecting a few significant events from the many that occur in the time span of the story and combining them in a significant and interesting way. Rather than show you everything that happened over a six-day period, a narrative instead shows you 90 minutes worth of those events that the narrator (the screenwriter, the director, and anyone else who happens to be in the room during a script conference) thinks interesting and important for the telling of the film's story. How those narrated events are selected and combined is an important dimension of the meaning of a film.

The specific choice of scenes and of scene order that filmmakers make is called the narrative strategy of the film. A principle narrative strategy is the withholding of information to create a mystery for the audience. Narratives thrive on delayed delivery. For example, at the outset of *Michael Clayton*, someone tries to kill the main character. A mystery is created, and we in the audience do not have enough information to resolve it. Why would someone want to kill this man? Who is he anyway? The film's narrative then loops back in time to before the event with which the film begins, and by the time we reach that point in the action a second time, our perspective has widened, we have more information, and we understand why someone wanted to kill Michael. The narrative explains to us that he has made a decision to expose the corruption in the company for which he works. And the meaning of the scene with which the film opens changes from being a simple moment of narrative exposition or storytelling to being a moment of enlightenment and moral choice. It is the exact moment when Michael decides to act against the corrupt corporation. He finally sees things as his friend Arthur saw them before he was murdered. It is a classic moment of *peripeteia* or reversal, in which the one-way flow of a narrative suddenly turns and goes in a very different direction.

Another important element of narrative strategy in screenplay writing is the point of view from which the story is told. For example, *Michael Clayton* usually focuses on Michael. His life and his interactions with other characters occupy most of the scenes. His perspective or point of view is given priority. But occasionally the film cuts away to two other characters—Arthur Eden, a friend of Michael's who takes a moral stance against corruption and urges Michael to do the same, and Karen Crowder, the head of the corrupt corporation who orders Arthur's murder and the attempted murder of Michael. Those two parallel narratives haunt Michael's story in two ways. Arthur's story is like a taunt against Michael. Arthur is a closer friend of Michael's son than Michael is because Arthur pays attention to the stories of knights and heroic quests that fascinate the son. Arthur also takes a stand against injustice. Unlike Michael, he has moral courage. Karen Crowder haunts Michael's story because she is the nemesis whose actions in the background lie outside Michael's range of knowledge. Only in the end does he deduce that she is responsible for Arthur's death. And his act of moral heroism consists of exposing her. So the three narrative strands—the main one that follows Michael's life and the two ancillary ones—end up being connected in important ways for the meaning of the film. The narrative perspective is centered on Michael throughout, and only in the end

FIGURES 5.1 & 5.2 *Michael Clayton.* Michael's story is woven together with that of two other characters who serve as thematic poles that measure his moral stature.

do we realize how the seemingly parallel stories of Karen and of Arthur have a bearing on his story.

Narratives are often constructed as movements of progress from negative to positive states. Characters evolve from conditions of weakness, moral blindness, or subordination to various states of rebirth, strength, moral redemption, or independence. In *The Silence of the Lambs* (1991), for example, Clarice moves from a condition of fallibility to one of accomplishment. During her FBI training sessions, she is depicted making mistakes that could be fatal, such as walking into a room and being blind-sided by a man with a gun. During the course of the film, she learns from Hannibal Lecter how to think properly so as to solve crimes. She finds a serial killer, and she graduates from the FBI academy. That transformation is coded as a passage from weakness and vulnerability to strength and competence. This larger narrative movement from fallibility to strength is repeated several times in smaller narratives within the larger one. At one point, for example, she goes to a hospital for the criminally insane to interview Lecter. On her way out, an inmate flings semen at her, and she becomes upset outside the prison building. Her sense of vulnerability triggers a memory of her father, who was a police officer. That memory seems to make her realize she must overcome her emotions and master her fears if she is to succeed. So the next shot is of her shooting a gun at the camera. She has stopped being upset, and has begun to adopt the tough identity the FBI provides.

Many movies are classic heroic narratives. They tell the story of a single individual who defeats a threat to a community to which s/he belongs. Such heroic narratives usually pose a simple model of heroic virtue against an equally simple model of villainous vice. The hero embodies norms we all share, while the villain usually breaches those norms and violates the basic rules of civilization such as respect for life and property. In the end, predictably, the heroic respecter of norms triumphs.

FIGURES 5.3 – 5.5 *The Silence of the Lambs*. In this sequence Clarice is overcome with emotion but then is shown learning to channel her emotions into focused violent action.

Classic narratives have been around for a long time, and they derive from oral folktales. Vladimir Propp studied such folktales and came up with a list of actions, events, or "functions" that they all contain (http://faculty.gvsu.edu/websterm/Hero.htm). Here they are:

1.   One of the members of a family absents himself from home.
2.   An interdiction (ban) is addressed to the hero.
3.   The interdiction is violated. (The villain usually enters the story here.)
4.   The villain makes an attempt at reconnaissance.

5. The villain receives information about his victim. (The villain gets an answer.)
6. The villain attempts to deceive his victim by using persuasion, magic, or deception.
7. The victim submits to deception and thereby unwittingly helps his enemy. (Hero sleeps.)
8. The villain causes harm or injury to a member of a family.
8a. One member of a family either lacks something or desires to have something.
9. Misfortune or lack is made known: the hero is approached with a request or command; he is allowed to go or he is dispatched.
10. The seeker (hero) agrees to or decides upon counteractions.
11. The hero leaves home.
12. The hero is tested, interrogated, attacked, etc., which prepares the way for his receiving either a magical agent or helper. (The donor usually enters the story here.)
13. The hero reacts to the actions of the future donor.
14. The hero acquires the use of a magical agent.
15. The hero is transferred, delivered, or led to the whereabouts of an object of search.

Either Path A: Struggle and Victory over Villain; End of Lack and Return:
16. The hero and villain join in direct combat.
17. The hero is branded.
18. The villain is defeated.
19. The initial misfortune or lack is liquidated.
20. The hero returns.
21. The hero is pursued.
22. The hero is rescued from pursuit.

Or Path B: Unrecognized Arrival, Task, Recognition, Punishment, Wedding:
23. The hero, unrecognized, arrives home or in another country.
24. A false hero presents unfounded claims.
25. A difficult task is proposed to the hero. (Trial by drink, fire, riddle, test of strength.)
26. The task is resolved or accomplished.
27. The hero is recognized, often by a mark or an object.
28. The false hero or villain is exposed and / or punished.
29. The hero is given a new appearance.
30. The villain is pursued.
31. The hero is married and ascends the throne.

The Searchers is a classic heroic narrative that follows Propp's outline. It is about a man who searches for his niece, who has been kidnapped by Native Americans. Ethan, an older white man, and Marty, a younger man who is half white and half Native, set out on a quest to find Debbie, a girl taken by Natives led by Chief Scar. Scar makes her one of his wives. After many years of searching, the men find her, kill Scar, and bring Debbie home.

In keeping with Propp's protocol, Ethan is initially absent from home. While his brother Aaron is a law-abiding homesteader, Ethan is presented as a law-breaker, someone associated with the Confederacy during the Civil War, who continues to steal money from the federal government. So he is associated with the breach of an interdiction in Propp's list of functions.

He and other members of the community are lured away from home by news of a Native raid that stole cattle. While they are away, the villain, Scar, reconnoiters Aaron's house, kills most of the family, and kidnaps Debbie and her sister. Ethan realizes that he has been deceived. The Indian raid was not to steal cattle but to murder and kidnap. He has unwittingly helped his enemy by riding out uselessly to look for cattle that the Natives have killed.

FIGURE 5.6 *The Searchers*. The hero, Ethan, realizes he has been deceived and unwittingly helped the villain. Notice how visually diminished he looks in the image.

Back home, Ethan is approached with a request to help Reverend Clayton find the girls. Clayton is also head of the Texas Rangers. Ethan sets out with the Rangers to find the girls. In Propp's terminology, he once again leaves home. Eventually, he and Marty search alone for Debbie. They receive news of her whereabouts from a donor. After a fight with Scar's band, during which he is pursued, Ethan is wounded ("branded"). Ethan and Marty now return home "unrecognized." No one is waiting for them or expects them. A false hero appears who wants to marry Marty's girlfriend. Marty, the new hero now that

Ethan is wounded, defeats the false hero, his girlfriend's suitor, in a ritual boxing match. Another version of a false hero now appears, a US Cavalry soldier who announces that Scar's band is camped nearby. An old friend, Moses Harper, is brought in to the house by the cavalrymen. He is mildly mad, and he speaks in riddles. No one can understand him. But Marty takes on the task and solves the riddle of where the Native camp is. Marty receives a new appearance when he takes off his clothes so he looks more like a Native. He enters Scar's camp, kills Scar, and frees Debbie. Marty returns home with Debbie and marries his girlfriend.

FIGURES 5.7 & 5.8 *The Searchers*. The opening shot is repeated at the end of the movie in this classic heroic narrative.

The film is a remarkable rendering of Propp's functions. But why would the stories we tell each other follow the same pattern over and over again? You'd think we would be a bit more innovative. It may be that the basic format of the hero narrative has something to do with our need to reinforce the basic norms of our culture and of our civilization.

The film concerns a conflict between civilization, which is associated with living by norms that come from law and religion (embodied in the character of Reverend Clayton), and animal nature, which is associated with the breaking of norms regarding such things as marriage and property ownership (associated with the Native chief Scar). The repetition in the narrative of movements of setting out and returning home suggests something that is enduring in human life (that repeats over time) but that needs to be constantly reiterated to take hold (much as one repeats something to memorize and learn it). That structure of narrative repetition is appropriate for a movie about the basic institutions, such as property, marriage, and family, that sustain civilization. They can only endure if they are reiterated or repeated in each new generation. The basic institutions and norms of civilization are restored to their intact state by the end of the movie. Given the theme of restoration, it is fitting that the narrative itself forms a circle. It begins with an image of a door being opened and ends with a similar image of a door being closed. In each shot, the camera shoots from inside the home because the domestic world is what is at stake in the film. That world is initially violated, but in the end, its identity is restored.

You will still see many instances of the classic heroic narrative in movie theaters. It remains a popular form of narrative storytelling. But you will also see movies that do not celebrate the power and virtue of a single hero. Some movies try to be more realistic and to depict flawed characters. They usually tell the story differently from classic narratives and do not follow a progressive temporal model.

Some films rearrange normal narrative continuity to make a point. For example, *Before the Devil Knows You're Dead* is about a breakdown of moral order, and the narrative is broken in a similar way. The fragmented narrative gives a better, more accurate portrait of the world depicted. Norms are abandoned as two brothers plot a robbery of their parents' jewelry store. The story is told out of sequence, and it is broken down into parts, each of which is told from the perspective of a different character. This narrative form seems appropriate to so broken a world.

The fragmented narrative form also embodies the idea that our actions have repercussions that sometimes exceed our intentions. By depicting the world from different perspectives, the filmmakers also show us the way intended actions affect others in unintended ways. It portrays why responsibility is so important a category in ethics. We are responsible for the effects of our actions on others. And we are therefore responsible in making moral decisions not just to ourselves and to our own sense of right and wrong but also to the people whose lives are affected by our actions. The film makes this point by distributing the perspective from which the story is told across several characters. The audience is obliged thereby to experience the effects of one character's actions on other characters.

ANDY: 4 DAYS BEFORE THE ROBBERY

FIGURE 5.9 *Before the Devil Knows You're Dead.* A fragmented narrative moves from one moment in time to another in the past.

Narrative perspective is the point of view from which a story is told. It is the position from which you see things in a film, and in a sense it obliges you to see the world in a particular way. Every film is made from a perspective. Perspective structures what will be seen both in the entire film and in each shot; it shapes meaning; and it determines whose values the audience will be invited to endorse. For example, *Iron Man* (2008) operates from a conservative American perspective and opens with a segment that obliges the viewer to see Arabs as torturers of Americans (at a time in history when, in fact, Americans were torturing Arabs). *Avatar* is told from a liberal, anti-capitalist, and pro-environmental Canadian perspective. As a result, the way the world looks is different from how the world appears in a movie like *Iron Man*. The corporate businessman of *Avatar* is corrupt and unpleasant; the one in *Iron Man* is charming and virtuous. Those harmed by capitalism are central agents in *Avatar*; in *Iron Man*, capitalism does no harm; instead, it saves the world.

Perspective places the audience in alignment with values associated with a particular point of view. For two hours you in the audience see the world as others see it, and the world you see varies quite a bit depending on the perspective. In most conservative crime melodramas, for example, poor people and people of color are portrayed as dangerous and devoid of moral values. Films like *Ransom* (1996) assume the perspective of wealthy white upper-middle-class people. Their perspective is privileged, and their values are endorsed. Usually such films suggest that ethnically dark-skinned, working-class others are threats who should be feared. For example, in this sequence from *Falling Down* (1993), a group of young Latino men taunt a hard-working white American, whose perspective is endorsed in the movie. He is portrayed as calm and reasonable, while they are portrayed as animalistic predators.

FIGURES 5.10 & 5.11 *Falling Down*. A white man is portrayed as rational and in control, while Latino youths are portrayed as animalistic and dangerous.

How the entire world of a movie looks, therefore, is determined by the perspective it operates from. And that perspective contains embedded values. To get a sense of how crucial perspective is for constructing cinematic worlds, imagine *The Silence of the Lambs* told from the murderer's point of view. Would it be possible? If it were, you'll admit it would be a very different looking cinematic world. In the existing film, the murderer, Jamie Gumm, is a projection rather than a plausibly real figure. Indeed, he seems like an intolerant heterosexual's fear-filled fantasy of a gay person. If the story were told from Jamie's perspective, one of the first things that would change, then, is that he would become more realistic and less fantastic. He might be a killer still, but why would a gay person kill? He might do so because he was tormented and abused by heterosexual men for being gay. In a film story told from his perspective, he might exact revenge on an intolerant heterosexist world by slaughtering those who abuse others. Rather than appear evil, he might appear to be a misguided avenging angel.

Writers who are called "postmodern" often take issue with the standard cause and effect format of narrative, and often draw attention to the way perspective works to limit knowledge. *Memento* (2000) is a well-known example of a postmodern film that eschews the traditional temporal progression of narrative and tells its story from end to beginning, moving backwards through time. *Atonement* (2007) is about the difference in perspective between child and adult, and it structures its moral tale around the way things change when seen from different perspectives. A child, Briony, attempts to understand a love affair her older sister, Cecilia, is engaged in with Bobby, a young man who does gardening at their country house. She finds the two of them making love and is so upset that, later in the evening, when two young boys get lost, she says she saw Bobby commit a crime he did not commit. He is put in jail and sent off to war where he is killed. The crossing of a child's perspective with an adult perspective is captured in the crime she witnesses—the rape of a girl her own age by an adult man who is visiting the house.

The film draws attention to the difference in meaning between adult events as they are lived and such events as seen from a child's perspective. Briony sees Bobby and Cecilia through a window arguing by a fountain out on the lawn far from the house. She can't hear what they are saying, but she is shocked by something that we do not see, and stops looking. When she looks again, Cecilia is getting dressed and is sodden wet. We in the audience are obliged to see things from her perspective. We hear nothing of what was said so that we could understand the meaning of the adult events. As a result, we get a truncated version that elides nakedness and the possibility of sexuality. Later, we see the same events as they occurred and understand them fully from this new perspective. The elision of reality and the incomprehension are important because they prepare the later scene when Briony witnesses the rape. Her limited perspective in this scene is suggested by her flashlight that only illuminates part of what is happening. When she herself is an adult, she is finally able to see what happened, to remember accurately that it was not Bobby who committed the crime. Her perspective is different now. She herself has briefly loved and lost, so she can adopt the perspective of the adults whose lives had baffled her as a child.

FIGURES 5.12 & 5.13 *Atonement.* A child who misinterprets the adult world is associated ironically with windows that seem to offer vision but instead promote misunderstanding.

Student Assignment: *Thelma and Louise* (1991)

Past classic narratives concerned male heroes. Do Propp's functions appear in a film about female heroes like *Thelma and Louise*?

Student Assignment: *Before the Devil Knows You're Dead*
(1.12.40 to 1.14.54)

Analyze the segment in terms of narrative fragmentation. How do the break and the shift in the narrative work? How is it significant?

Student Assignment: *M* (1931) (59:14 to 1:01:06)

What kinds of assumptions can we make about this film from this short sequence? Who are these characters and what are they doing? Consider in particular the concepts of perspective and point of view covered earlier in this section: describe the uses of these techniques—how are they utilized in these sequences and to what end?

FIGURE 5.14 *M*. In this famous silent film, a serial killer stalks a child.

FURTHER READING

Bordwell, David. *The Way Hollywood Tells It: Story and Style in Modern Movies.* Berkeley: University of California Press, 2006.

Chatman, Seymour. *Coming to Terms: The Rhetoric of Narrative in Fiction and Film.* Ithaca: Cornell University Press, 1990.

Propp, V. *Morphology of the Folktale.* Austin: University of Texas Press, 1968.

Ryan, Marie-Laure. *Narrative Across Media: the Languages of Storytelling.* Lincoln: University of Nebraska Press, 2004.

Thompson, Kristin. *Storytelling in Film and Television.* Cambridge: Harvard University Press, 2003.

Van Peer, Willie, and Seymour Chatman. *New Perspectives on Narrative Perspective.* Albany: State University of New York Press, 2001.

Van Sijill, Jennifer. *Cinematic Storytelling.* Studio City: Michael Weise Productions, 2005.

Metaphor, Structure, Character, Motif

Meaning in movies is also created through metaphor, structure, character, and motifs. In a metaphor, a thing is associated with an idea or an emotional state. Structure describes the overall design of a movie, the way different elements balance one another. Characters are created by screenwriters and given life by actors. Their development—from ignorance to enlightenment or fear to courage—is often a way of making meaning in movies. Finally, meaning is created through motifs or repetitive elements such as objects that evoke themes, feelings, or ideas.

Metaphors make meaning by comparing two different things. They often link characters to objects within the same image. For example, in this image, a war veteran who has lost his job and his wife is compared visually to scrapped airplanes no longer needed now that the war has been won.

FIGURE 6.1 *The Best Years of Our Lives.* A man is compared to scrapped airplanes in this metaphoric image.

The image from *The Best Years of Our Lives* creates a metaphoric association between the airplanes and Fred, himself a leftover no one apparently wants. Shot by themselves, the airplanes might simply have had value as information: a lot of planes were made and are no longer needed now that the war is over. Shot alone in an empty field, Fred might have been portrayed as lonely and rejected, an unemployed divorcee. But when the two pieces are put together within the same frame, a metaphor is created. Soldiers, the image infers, are like scrapped airplanes that no one wants. They helped win the war, but are now disposable. The metaphor makes a stronger argument than either visual element alone would have made in a single frame on its own.

Metaphoric associations also help tell stories by communicating information about a character's inner emotional state. In these images, from the opening sequence of *Mildred Pierce*, Mildred walks across a dock toward the water. We don't realize yet that she is contemplating suicide. As she approaches the rail on the wharf, Mildred looks down at the water, which is roiled and swirls, seemingly, around her head. The metaphoric association between the disturbed water and her disturbed emotional state is obvious, but, on another level of meaning, the water emblemizes the fluid dissolution of boundaries that Mildred represents. She cannot maintain clear personal boundaries between herself and her daughter, Veda, and Mildred allows crossed personal and emotional

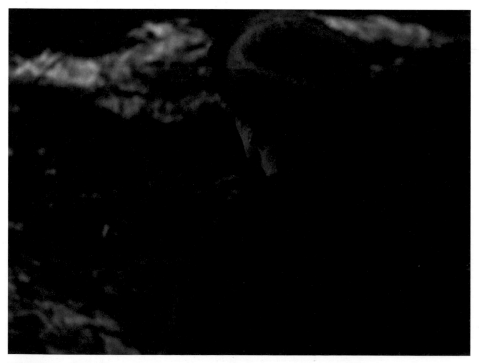

FIGURES 6.2 *Mildred Pierce*. In this image, water is a metaphor for emotional confusion.

boundaries to undermine the clear line between right and wrong in the eyes of the law.

Nature metaphors are often used in movies to suggest states of being the filmmakers endorse. Nature is often associated with authenticity, spontaneity, and truthfulness. We trust authentic people who speak the truth and distrust false people whose statements are empty and artificial. Nature imagery is thus often juxtaposed to images connoting artificiality and falseness. In *Klute*, images of nature are juxtaposed to images of the city, and life in the city is portrayed as artificial. John Klute, a detective, searches for the murderer of a friend with the help of Bree Daniels, a sex worker. The filmmakers suggest through the association of Klute with nature that he is authentic and that his values are good. Bree, on the other hand, is linked to constructed environments that appear cool and inhuman. If Klute's link to

FIGURE 6.3 *Klute*. Nature is linked to a benevolent vision of the family.

FIGURE 6.4 *Klute*. The city acts as a metaphor for alienation and loss of identity and is associated with anonymous sexual relations.

FIGURE 6.5 *Michael Clayton*: Michael's friend, Arthur, is depicted as being superior to Michael.

images of nature suggests personal and moral authenticity, Bree's association with the city evokes the idea of artificiality and anonymity. She aspires to be an actress, and as a sex worker she acts out parts with her clients, who are nameless, faceless people with whom she avoids personal exposure. In one image, a customer is depicted without a head, while in another, Bree is juxtaposed to a mannequin. She is portrayed as lacking a real or natural identity of her own.

All movies are carefully designed, and they all have structure. That means that the elements of a movie complement one another. For example, characters with different qualities or values balance one another. In *Michael Clayton*, Michael is juxtaposed to his friend Arthur, who has decided to oppose the immorality of the law firm for which they both work. The structure of this film resides in the way two characters with two very different moral qualities are posed against one another.

Arthur is first presented as a rule-breaker, someone who has gone mad. But it quickly becomes clear that the film is drawing on an old meaning of madness as religious enlightenment and inspiration. The audience usually laughs at one point when Arthur, responding to Michael's attempt to remind him that he is a lawyer with responsibilities, says "I am Shiva the Destroyer." And at another point, evoking the parable of the loaves and fishes from the New Testament, he is pictured carrying a large bag of bread.

The working out of this structure of ideas and characters is aided by a familiar metaphoric opposition between nature and artifice. Michael is connected to natural creatures like horses, while his adversary, Karen Crowder, the head of the corrupt agri-business corporation, is linked to mirrors and acting. She is depicted rehearsing lines she will later deliver at meetings—pretending they are spontaneous and authentic and unrehearsed. Michael, in contrast, is shown speaking the plain truth to people who would prefer not to hear it. In the structure of the film, Karen is a corrupt liar who occupies one pole, while Arthur is at the other pole as someone willing to speak truth to power. Initially Michael is in the middle. He arranges to protect people who step outside the norms of society or who breach the basic rules of civilization. And those actions place him closer to Karen in the structure of the film. But, in the end, he shifts towards Arthur and reveals the truth about the corporation's malfeasance. Fittingly, this occurs in a scene in which he confronts Karen, the representative of all he opposes by this point in the film.

While structure describes the architecture of a movie, motifs are more like a thread of a different color from the main fabric that runs through a movie. A motif appears occasionally, usually in passing. A motif can be a thing, a sound, an image, or any other evocative and meaningful thematic element. For example, religion is a motif in *Amelie*. The film was made in France, and in French culture the Catholic Church has exercised enormous influence. In the movie, religion is associated with excess order and with the attempt to control one's destiny by making it immune to chance. Amelie's mother tries to control fate by lighting prayer candles at Notre Dame cathedral to aid her in having

FIGURES 6.6 & 6.7 *Michael Clayton*. Michael is associated with nature, while Karen, his adversary, is associated with mirrors and rehearsed speeches.

a son. But, as she leaves the cathedral, she is killed by someone committing suicide by jumping from the roof. Chance defeats the mother's effort to control destiny.

Amelie herself lives a cloistered life. She is shy and introverted, and she lives retired from the world, like a nun. In one sequence that takes place in an old Metro station in Paris called "Les Abbesses" (the term for nuns who are in charge of Catholic abbeys), she encounters a blind man playing an old love song on a phonograph. The images on the wall are advertisements that contain

FIGURES 6.8 *Amelie.* Religion is a motif running through this French film

FIGURE 6.9 *Chungking Express.* Visual information furthers the ends of characterization.

images of nature and of fruit, but, like Amelie herself, the fruitfulness they represent is contained and muted—a "still life," or a "*nature morte*" to use the French expression for a still life painting evoked by one character in the film. The stilling of nature is linked to the idea of being an abbess, like Amelie. Fittingly, near the end, when several characters, including Amelie, become more flexible and open to the risks of existence, a group of Benedictine monks are shown playing a game of shuttlecocks. The religious motif in the film concludes its run with an image of religious stricture giving way to flexibility, play, and chance.

Student Assignment: *High and Low* (1963)

Akira Kurosawa's film is a moral tragedy that concerns the decision Gondo must make when his chauffeur's son is kidnapped in place of his own son. Should he give his wealth to the chauffeur to rescue his son? Consider the depiction of the criminal and the final encounter between him and Gondo before he is executed. How does the film link class difference to criminality? How is Gondo characterized?

Student Assignment: *Chungking Express* (1994) (56:57 to 1:00:02)

Although these two sequences are brief, a great deal of information can be gleaned from them. Using the language from this chapter, describe the sequences thoroughly. Now consider: what do these scenes tell us about the characters of "Cop 663" and Faye? What kinds of things does each character value and how do you know?

FURTHER READING

Blumenfield, Robert. *Tools and Techniques for Character Interpretation*. Pompton Plains: Limelight Editions, 2006.

Britton, Pers. *Reading Between Designs: Visual Imagery and the Generation of Meaning*. Austin: The University of Texas Press, 2003.

Fuery, Patrick, and Kelli Fuery. *Visual Cultures and Critical Theory*. London: Arnold, 2003.

Knowles, Murray. *Introducing Metaphor*. London: Routledge, 2006.

Krasner, David. *Method Acting Reconsidered*. New York: St. Martin's Press, 2000.

Leighton, John. *1,100 Designs and Motifs from Historic Sources*. New York: Dover, 1995.

Rose, Brian. *An Examination of Narrative Structure in Four Films of Frank Capra*. New York: Arno Press, 1980.

Tan, Ed. *Emotion and the Structure of Narrative Film*. Hillsdale: Erlbaum Associates, 1996.

Walker, Michael. *Hitchcock's Motifs*. Amsterdam: Amsterdam University Press, 2005.

Film Style: Realism and Expressionism

Most films are told in a realist style. They aspire to appear to record real life as it happens before your eyes, as if you were looking through a window. Others use high contrast lighting and highly metaphoric images in an expressionist style that appears more laden with visual meaning. Such films seek to *express* psychological states or moral conditions in images. Whenever you see a screen image in which the characters are completely blackened out, you are watching expressionism at work.

That you can choose how to depict the world should tell you how much choice goes into any image on the screen. Every technical decision in filmmaking distinguishes between possible worlds. The world can be represented as dark and threatening or as bright and cheery. Each approach to filmmaking evokes a different mood and different ideas in the audience. But if the world can be represented in so many different ways, how do we know which images of it are true or accurate?

Filmmakers in the documentary and the experimental filmmaking communities think about that question quite a bit. They are concerned with how we represent reality and with how the images or representations we use both help and hinder our quest to portray the world as it truly is. For example, the

FIGURES 7.1 & 7.2 *The Best Years of Our Lives* and *Out of the Past* (1947). The two basic film styles—realism and expressionism—generate very different visual images.

"reality" that a documentary captures is formed by the documentary filmmaker's choice of shots and editing decisions, and it is often formed with rhetorical ends in mind. That is, it tries to convince you of something or to affect how you view the world. Most documentaries strive to have a significant effect on the audience, and they do so by converting the elements of the real that they capture on film into arguments about the world. Real people become like fictional characters; real events have "plots"; and actuality is filmed with a final cinematic image in mind. To capture the real in documentary is to bend it to the final rhetorical purpose of the film. The real becomes artistic, as much a matter of form as of fact.

Michael Moore's *Roger and Me* (1989) is a good example of the forming of reality for rhetorical purposes. The film is organized as a quest narrative, but "finding the corporate head" replaces "finding the girl" as the motivating source of the plotting. Moore sets out to find Roger Smith, the head of General Motors, to invite him to spend a day in Flint, Michigan, a city recently devastated by GM plant closings that Smith engineered. He moved production out of the US to lower-wage countries, thus permitting GM to expand into more lucrative enterprises. Investors profited; American workers lost their livelihoods; and Flint, Michigan, was destroyed.

Moore draws on classical rhetorical resources such as repetition, juxtaposition, pathos, exaggeration, plea, and polemic to make the point that men like Smith live well in a comfortable, insulated world apart from the impoverished reality they create when they behave callously for the sake of their own gain. Moore contextualizes Smith by evoking numerous examples of desolation from the world Smith both creates and ignores. The most forceful motif Moore uses is the juxtaposition of repeated images of people being evicted from their homes to images of leisure and wealth (rich women playing golf and saying how good life in Flint is). Moore's point is that Smith and others live well and enjoy wealth at the same time that they use a claim of economic hardship to fire workers and save costs. He argues that such actions impose huge costs on local communities even as they seemingly save money for a wealthy few.

Jenny Livingston's *Paris is Burning* (1990) is a documentary in which the reality of the "real" is in question. It concerns voguing, the practice of competing at dressing up as someone else, often a particular type of person such as an executive or a college student. The participants in the vogue balls are usually gay and either black or Hispanic. Some are transvestites or cross-dressers in real life. The film follows certain "characters," such as Willi Ninja, who becomes successful as a vogue dancer, and Venus Extravaganza, a cross-dresser who is saving up money for a sex change operation but who is murdered by the end of the movie.

In a culture characterized by intolerance towards homosexuality, homosexuals are obliged to live in the "closet," a metaphor for keeping their gender identities hidden from the dominant heterosexual population. They must "pass" as heterosexuals. The voguing the film depicts is a metaphor for this quite real issue of having to pretend to be "normal" or

FIGURES 7.3 & 7.4 *Roger and Me*. Michael Moore uses canny juxtapositions in this documentary.

to dress a part in order to survive in an intolerant mono-sexual culture. The film cuts away from the balls at certain point to portray "normal" men and women on the street. The effect of these images is to provoke one to rethink the relationship in mainstream or majoritarian heterosexual culture between dress and gender identity. The most interesting vogue competition is organized around "realness," the attempt to perfectly imitate a particular identity such as executive or soldier. This competition of course raises the question of what it means for something to be real as opposed to imitation. How is the reality of the real constituted? Are the men and women on the

FIGURES 7.5 & 7.6 *Paris is Burning*. This film compares gay cross-dressers with "real" people.

street in real identities as opposed to vogued ones? If so, why do they all dress alike? They would all seem to be imitating the same model, wearing the same uniform. The film makes its critique more emphatic by depicting some of the cross-dressed characters on the street intermingling with people who "really" inhabit their identity; the two groups are of course indistinguishable. Even more compelling is a sequence in which a gay cross-dresser teaches heterosexual women how to walk like real women. How, the film suggests, can gender identity be considered real when imitators teach real people to behave like "themselves"?

Most mainstream films tend to reinforce the standing order of society—the norms, practices, and institutions that those with power to determine such things proclaim and assume to be necessary, true, and real. Such films respect whatever morality is paramount, reinforce whatever order of gender relations exists, and hew to whatever economic lay-out counts as reality-as-it-must-be-and-always-will-be. If mainstream films tend to reinforce the assumptions of the audience, experimental filmmakers such as Maya Deren in *Meshes of the Afternoon* (1943) and Kenneth Anger in *Scorpio Rising* (1964) challenge those assumptions. That in part explains why they often resort to representational forms and methods that depart from or undermine the norms of narrative filmmaking. Experimental filmmakers often work outside the standing order (Deren because she was a female filmmaker at a time when the industry had become almost exclusively male after multi-gendered beginnings, and Anger because he was gay at a time when heterosexuality was the unquestioned norm of American culture). *Meshes of the Afternoon*, for example, takes place within a dream, allowing its characters to behave in unexpected ways; they drift through space and change appearance. Deren's view of her position in relation to mainstream filmmakers may be reflected by the characters' abilities to control reality-based events—even death—from within their dream world. Anger's *Scorpio Rising* could only have been an experimental movie at the time at which it was made. It celebrates the gay community and mockingly evokes the stereotypes of mainstream hetero-sexual culture. Images of gay motorcyclists are juxtaposed to clips from a religious movie about Jesus Christ while the song "He's A Rebel" plays on the sound track.

Alternative or experimental cinema challenges the hegemonic position of realism in mainstream film production in a number of ways. It approximates lyric poetry, the creation of meaning through the juxtaposition of images in a way that departs from the usual plot protocols of narration. It works against identification with character. And it involves the audience generally on a more intellectual level than mainstream narratives. If narrative fictions ask us to think once, to accept the seen as real, experimental films often ask us to think twice, to reflect on the way the real and the image mutually determine one another. It is this consideration of the act of viewing that encourages viewers to be aware that what we see in everyday perception is a mixture of "reality" or events in the world and our own cognitive processes for perceiving those events.

FIGURES 7.7 & 7.8 *Scorpio Rising*. In this celebration of the gay counterculture of California in the 1960s, Jesus Christ's rebelliousness is compared to that of gay motorcyclists.

If the experimental cinema often questions the regimes of perception and cognition that prevent us from seeing the world around us more critically, mainstream narrative cinema often tends towards platitudes designed to please a mass audience and to reinforce their assumptions about the world (the redemption of a bad character, the successful attainment of a goal, finding the girl, etc.). The audience comes away from the cinematic experience feeling that the world is as it is the only way it can be; it is "real" and therefore it has the weight of something permanent and unquestioned. By simply depicting action that occurs within the realm of the "real," mainstream narrative film assigns that world a quality of unquestionability that it may not deserve. The most obviously dubious example of such assignment would be a film like *Birth of a Nation* (1915) that assumes a reality in which African-Americans deserve lynching if they seek voting rights.

In the world of mainstream cinema, problems can be cleared up through virtuous effort on the part of a few heroic people. Our institutions can correct themselves. Genre films (the western, the action adventure, the melodrama, etc.) are especially prone to supporting such assumptions because they are especially predictable in their use of formal conventions (the hero sets out on a quest and succeeds; a relationship falls apart but a redemptive resolution occurs, etc.). Such generic redundancy and repetition reinforces the sense that the current state of things in the world is sound and good and "real"; our assumptions about it are justified; we can take "reality" for granted, no matter how much violence, domination, injustice, and corruption it harbors within it. By disturbing the way cinematic reality is normally constructed in mainstream narrative films, experimental films made under the banner of the alternative cinema disturb that sense of certainty regarding reality. For this reason, they are often anti-generic. They summon the conventions and the platitudes only to subvert them and to disturb the sense of comfort and certainty the conventions and platitudes usually provide.

Alan Resnais's *Hiroshima, Mon Amour* (1965) seeks to disturb that complacency by mixing genres and importing to the mode and style of fictional narrative features of more compellingly realistic forms such as the documentary. The film begins poetically with near still images of twined bodies, but those lovers' bodies quickly blend into bodies that resemble those of victims of the atomic bomb at Hiroshima in 1945. The two lovers, one French and the other Japanese, discuss whether one can know something like Hiroshima, with the Japanese man assuring the French woman that one cannot, as the screen is filled with images of the Hiroshima museum and of the aftermath of the blast. He compares the knowledge of such an atrocity to love because both kinds of knowledge are filled with delusion.

The film's point, that one cannot (and should not) forget the past, becomes a feature of its own composition. The story moves between the present and flashbacks to the past when the French woman fell in love with a German soldier, was punished, and fled to Paris. In normal generic films about such issues as war, "enemies" usually remain unknown and unknowable, and, as a result, they remain in personal opposition, objects

FIGURES 7.9 & 7.10 *Hiroshima, Mon Amour*. Director Alain Resnais threads documentary footage into his fictional story of a love affair between a French woman and a Japanese man.

rather than subjects, targets of our violence rather than collaborators at finding agreement or reconciliation. *Hiroshima* evokes these generic conventions by staging two love affairs by the same woman with two different "enemies," one Japanese, the other German. But her love for them also hollows out those generic conventions and reveals them to also be social and cognitive conventions. We go to war because of how we represent others to ourselves. We can choose, the film suggests, to have them be "enemies" or lovers.

Contemporary filmmaking exploits the lessons of the experimental cinema. *2046* is an unconventional love story that uses an unconventional narrative style. Wong Kar-Wai tells the story episodically, elliptically, and indirectly. Rather than engage in narrative exposition by showing an event, he will allude to it or show its result. Feelings are conveyed through minor gestures. And rather than follow the usual generic convention of a single successful quest romance (as in, say, *Fifty First Dates* (2004), a classic

FIGURES 7.11 & 7.12 *2046.* Wong Kar-Wai draws on the resources of the experimental cinema in off-center compositions and in fantasy image segments.

generic example), Wong chooses instead to portray failure through a series of happenstance, contingently related moments. The narrative blends fantasy segments with realist segments that draw attention to how we infuse reality with our feelings, dreams, and aspirations even as we seek to know it "as it is." Wong constructs images that displace the centrality of characters and make their perspective less certain, their perceptions less sure. In a number of images, characters are pushed to the side of the frame, or their faces are obscured by objects or other characters. The certainty of success and virtue in normal realist genre films is thereby undermined in this story of unsuccessful love.

Student Assignment: *Inside Job* (2010)

How is this film structured as a narrative? How does it tell its story? What cinematic devices such as composition, camera work, and editing does it use? What strategies does it employ to convince you of the reality of the point it makes?

Student Assignment: *History and Memory* (1991)

How does this film by Rea Tajiri rely on both narrative and lyric techniques to create meaning? How does the method of juxtaposition assist narrative construction? The film integrates documentary footage. What function does the footage serve? Finally, how is the fragmented style of the film appropriate to its theme?

Student Assignment: *The Tree of Life* (2011)

How does this film draw on the techniques and style of the experimental cinema? How does its method of story-telling advance its themes?

FIGURES 7.13 & 7.14 *Tree of Life*. This film draws on the visual language of the experimental cinema to tell a story of personal loss.

FURTHER READING

Aufderheide, Patricia. *Documentary Film*. New York: Oxford University Press, 2007.

Geiger, Jeffrey. *American Documentary Film*. Edinburgh: Edinburgh University Press, 2011.

Hatfield, Jackie. *Experimental Film and Video: An Anthology*. Bloomington: Indiana University Press, 2006.

O'Pray, Michael. *Avant Garde Film: Forms, Themes, Passions*. New York: Wallflower, 2003.

Critical Analysis

INTRODUCTION

Movies mean in multiple ways. *Avatar* refers to an historically recent debate between corporate economic conservatism and liberal humanist environmentalism. It is very much about a particular economic model and a particular culture war. Moreover, it is about love and sexuality; it explores human psychology; and it poses and answers ethical questions having to do with loyalty and trust. The movie has no one meaning but is more like a multi-faceted crystal that shines light in multiple directions.

What is called "criticism" explores those multi-faceted meanings by isolating each one and exploring it in depth. To criticize a cultural object such as a movie is not to say negative things about it. It is rather to stand back from it, put on hold one's emotional involvement with the story, and analyze its various components so that one can see how they function together. A critical analysis of *Avatar* might begin with the obvious economic theme—the power of corporations to inflict harm on the world for profit. It might then connect that theme to its moment in history, when corporate power was a significant public issue. Further, it would explore how the different characters are portrayed in relation to that theme. They evidence different ethical positions that involve choices and differing senses of loyalty to different institutions (corporation or tribe, for example). And so on.

What follows in this book will introduce you to a comprehensive set of critical approaches to the analysis of film. They range from politics and economics to sexuality and evolutionary theory. You will receive a brief introduction to the major ideas of each approach, and then you will be shown how those ideas might apply to the analysis of a particular movie. Each chapter concludes with a student exercise.

Historical Criticism

A ll films bear the marks of the moment at which they were made, and, as a consequence, they are available for historical interpretation. Such interpretation would note how a film refers to its particular moment of history, the specific social situation in which it was made.

Consider the example of a film from the decade of the 1930s, the era of the Great Depression, which left many Americans jobless and homeless. The film— *The Gold Diggers of 1933*—deals with romance primarily, but it also concerns economic troubles. Most films are about a vague and undefined historical present, but *Gold Diggers* has a more emphatic historical index than most. The period of its production and release, from 1932 to the spring of 1933, witnessed a deepening of the Depression, which began in 1929 with the stock market crash. Herbert Hoover, the president since 1928, believed in leaving the economy alone to take care of itself, and this hands-off attitude seemed only to make matters worse. He was defeated in the election of 1932 by Franklin Roosevelt, who offered a much more optimistic vision and promised more aggressive remedial action on the part of government.

Hoover lost the election for several reasons. One was that he refused to offer assistance to people without money or jobs. An old-stock conservative, he believed that individuals were responsible for their own fates and that the poor should take care of themselves. Another reason was the way he handled a protest march on Washington by veterans of World War I who wanted the government to pay out bonus monies early that were due them at a later date. Thinking the Bonus March a Communist conspiracy, Hoover ordered the army to disperse the marchers. In the violence that ensued, several people died, and Hoover came to appear callous and uncaring. It is important that the marchers referred to themselves as "forgotten men," and that Roosevelt, sensing an advantage, used that same phrase to refer to the unemployed in general during his presidential campaign.

The film draws on this historical context in its references to "Forgotten Men" in the final musical number and by setting its story amongst the down and out. But it can also be interpreted as an argument in favor of Roosevelt's New Deal, with its generous programs of government assistance for the poor and unemployed. Although historians of the era like Alan Brinkley mistakenly consider such films to be mere escapism, *Gold Diggers* is very much about the economic policy debates of the era, especially the debate over President Franklin

Roosevelt's New Deal, which relied on government to aid the distressed and to spur the economy back to life. Many who opposed the New Deal called for a renewal of individual entrepreneurship as a means of generating jobs and wealth. Then as today, a crucial issue was taxes. One side favored high tax rates on the wealthy that would give the government money for needed programs to help the poor. The other side favored tax cuts to put money in the pockets of businessmen who would use it to invest in new economic activities. The movie takes the side of the government and the New Deal and argues for "deficit spending," the newly invented liberal idea that government should go into debt and spend borrowed money to spur the country out of the economic depression. Borrowing in order to spend money on job-creating activities was looked on skeptically by conservatives who felt you had to have real money in hand before you should spend any. Liberals were essentially advocating the idea of imaginary money, and that is what makes the opening segment of *Gold Diggers* so interesting historically. Showgirls on stage in bright costumes sing "We're in the Money," but the money is entirely imaginary. The show is instead shut down by hard-nosed policemen because it has no real money. The producer argues that if they would let the show go on—on borrowed money— it would produce enough income to pay off the debt—essentially the liberal New Deal argument of the time.

The film concerns a group of "showgirls," singers and actresses in Broadway musical shows who are down on their luck because of the Depression. But with the help of Brad, a Boston blue-blood who is inexplicably slumming in the city and who donates money, they put on a show about the Depression itself. Brad's wealthy older brother, Lawrence, and his friend Peabody, an old Boston patrician, show up and try to prevent Brad from marrying one of the girls, Polly. Armed with lots of upper-class prejudices regarding "gold diggers," girls who marry for money, they themselves end up falling in love with two of the showgirls. Lawrence falls in love with Carol, who pretends to be Brad's girlfriend Polly in order to get back at Lawrence for disparaging showgirls. Peabody falls for Trixie, whose name suggests what she is—a real trickster and gold digger. In the end, all the romantic couples are happily joined, and the movie concludes with the "Forgotten Man" number from the new show that Brad has financed, a plea for help for the unemployed veterans of World War I.

It might help to begin at the end of the film with the "Forgotten Man" musical number. Carol leans against a lamppost dressed as a prostitute and sings "Forgotten Man", which evokes images of World War I soldiers now without work and which is a plea on their behalf. A policeman appears and makes a poor man sitting in a doorway stand up and move on, but Carol intervenes and pulls back the man's lapel to reveal a World War I medal. To audiences at the time, this encounter would evoke memories of the Bonus March fiasco in Washington, and the film is clearly placing its sympathy with the marchers. Moreover, the fact that Carol is dressed as a prostitute evokes the possibility that if men are not given jobs, then their wives will have to prostitute themselves to support their families, and indeed, the number of arrests for prostitution did go up during this period. After this moment in the sequence, an African-American woman takes over singing for Carol, the orchestra joins in, and the camera pans from Carol to the new singer and then to a woman holding a child in an image reminiscent of the social realist photography being done at this time, a style of photography intended to make the sufferings of the poor more palpable for a national audience. Panning works to subliminally connect people and imply a sense of community between people of different stations and races.

FIGURE 8.1 *The Gold-Diggers of 1933*. A prostitute stands up for a down-and-out veteran in this film that argues in favor of the liberal New Deal social welfare programs of the 1930s designed to combat the Great Depression.

The sequence now shifts to images of soldiers marching home to cheering crowds and confetti, then standing in line waiting for handouts of bread and coffee. The contrast between the images of glory and the images of poverty suggests that, while the soldiers were treated as heroes when they came home from the war, now they are treated as bums. Interlaced with these images are images of wounded soldiers carrying each other that remind the audience of the price the soldiers paid on their behalf. In the hand-out line, the men pass cigarettes back and forth in a gesture that foregrounds an ideal of community and mutual help that the film endorses. Finally, the sequence concludes with Carol standing between a background of soldiers marching and a foreground of people turned towards her with outstretched arms and singing to the audience again. By now the song has become an explicit plea for assistance: "Oh won't you lend a hand to my forgotten man." The camera draws back to create an image of a large community or society of people, of which her individual case is only a part. The sequence has thus evolved from a tight close-up of her face, which individuates her suffering and draws attention to her particular pain, to a long, wide angle shot of her position within a larger group that shares her sense of suffering and joins in her plea for help. This act of generalization from the particular individual to the larger social group or community implicitly continues out into the film audience to whom the final plea is directed.

FIGURE 8.2 *The Gold Diggers of 1933.* The final image of the film evokes an ideal of community.

Few films constitute legislative pleas, but *Gold Diggers* might justifiably be characterized as one of them. It is as if it were directed not just at the usual kind of film audience but also at a national audience of people who might possibly influence legislators to create programs of assistance for the poor and unemployed. That rhetorical gesture is understandable given the historical moment of the film, at the point of transition between 1932, when the Depression was at its worst and Hoover was defeated by Roosevelt, and 1933, when Roosevelt assumed office and promised relief for the poor. The emphatic historical character of the final musical number would seem only to make the fluffiness of all that comes before more noticeable. But the romantic plots contribute to the film's plea.

They can be interpreted as portraying an overcoming of prejudices that stand in the way of generosity. Lawrence and his upper-class companion Peabody think of "showgirls" as "gold diggers" who latch on to rich men in order to take advantage of their wealth. The girls they mistake for Brad's would-be wife and friend are so offended by the men's expression of these prejudices that they set about fleecing the two wealthy Bostonians just for the fun of it. Trixie, the more worldly of the two showgirls, becomes an authentic gold digger, and the film makes much humor of her cynicism regarding money and how one gets it. But it also establishes a contrast with Carol, who falls in love quite authentically with Lawrence. When he offers her money after mistakenly thinking he has had drunken sex with her, she refuses it. Invested in the ideal of an authentic virtue that transcends material circumstances, the film presents her as someone who would rather remain poor than compromise her sense of her own innate moral value. Only when he realizes his mistake can he overcome his prejudice regarding showgirls and see her for what she is truly worth.

If we think of Lawrence and Peabody as representatives of the same social group as Hoover and the Republicans who supported him, the connections between the romantic plot and the film's political plea become clear. Like Hoover and the Republicans, Lawrence and Peabody are suspicious of the motives of poor people. They feel that when the poor ask for assistance, it is a trick to deprive them of their wealth. What the film depicts is a transformation whereby the two upper-class characters learn to trust the lower-class characters. They come to see them as hard-working and virtuous. The historical significance of the film can be said to lie in the lesson it offers to conservatives who opposed government help for the poor. They can be trusted, it argues. They are not out for a free ride. They are, given a chance, willing to work hard.

But what of Trixie, the true gold digger who fleeces Peabody? Her story would seem to confirm upper-class prejudices. She seems an embodiment of the cynicism many in the audience no doubt were feeling at the time in regard to money and personal morality. Many had reached a point of destitution and despair that probably made the cynical sacrifice of traditional moral principles for the sake of money both understandable and acceptable. Trixie in effect has to be there to lend weight and reality to the negative financial position of the showgirls. She represents a reality characterized by the abandonment of morality for the sake of physical survival. Trixie is in effect what Carol chooses not to be, and Carol's choice would not be visible or significant if the alternative to virtue were not depicted.

The film thus can be said to contain a second film that is more documentary in character and that has to do with the economic circumstances and debates of the period. The romance plot can be understood simultaneously as a story of the overcoming of cross-class misunderstanding. Given a break from above, the poor can rise, and a depressing economic failure can be turned into a success predicated on interclass trust and cooperation.

But how might the musical numbers, especially the first two, be understood from this perspective? During these musical interludes, the film seems to take a break from its historically tinged romantic story and engage in fabulous images with no apparent real or historical referent. Indeed, they very explicitly abandon all pretense to represent reality, in this case a real stage, by expanding visual space and introducing actions that could only occur in a film studio. At these points, the film seems to move beyond realism altogether into a plastic play space where all obligations to historical reality no longer have a role in shaping what might appear on screen.

Nevertheless, even this remarkable transcendence of history is historically inflected. For what all three numbers depict is a magical transformation of reality that is in keeping with the progressive and optimistic argument of the film. At the very moment Roosevelt was promising to change an economic reality that seemed unamenable to change, the film portrays a transformation of limited theatrical space into a cinematic space that allows a wider range of representation and image construction. The limitations of theatrical reality are overcome, and images are created that would have seem impossible to attain a few moments before. Beyond realism lie optimistic representational possibilities that seem to create realities of their own. The usual relationship between the real and theatrical representation is reversed.

FIGURE 8.3 *The Gold Diggers of 1933*. The musical numbers transcend the limitations of theatrical space.

This indeed was the argument of the New Deal: that the economic situation of the country was not a reality one had to live with because nothing could be done about it; rather, it could be changed with effort, imagination, and will. The political project would have to be an aesthetic one of refabrication and reconstruction that entailed reversing the normal relationship between economic "reality" and government (or political representation). In the past, especially in the business-friendly 1920s, the government represented the economy and did not behave as if it could presume to shape economic reality using artificial tools like the imaginary money of deficit spending. Now, the New Deal government was promising to use just such artificial tools as administrative agencies and deficit spending to reverse that relationship and determine the course of economic reality.

The camera work throughout also conspires to lend credence to the liberal outlook on life espoused by Roosevelt, an outlook that favored a communitarian ideal over the individualist-survivalist ideal Hoover and the conservative Republicans promoted. During the first number, the camera tracks across a park setting from one romantic couple to another. All are of different ages and professions and ethnicities, and the implication of the camera work is that they are all connected, all part of a community. The Hooverite image of the strong male individualist is undermined and superseded by camera work that suggests that people inhabit communities in which relations are as important as individuals.

Later, during the final number, the full resonance of that ideal will become more evident. After several tracking and pan shots that connect different people, the community bands together to address the audience with its appeal for assistance. Such assistance is only imaginable if one feels connected to others, and the camera work attempts to establish such a sense of connection. Moreover, a sense of empathy with others is possible only as an act of imagination, an ability to move beyond one's own cognitive limits (one's own reality) and enter others' lives. It would seem appropriate, then, that the musical numbers, those fantastic and imaginative departures from the mandate that they be held accountable to a represented reality, promote just such a sense of the possibility of transcending the limits of lived reality. And the unreal images created in those numbers would not be possible without coordinated, cooperative effort. They embody the film's communitarian ideal.

The liberal ideals that animate a film like *Gold Diggers* rest on a vision of the human personality as being flexible and relational and on a vision of virtue as helping others who are part of one's field of relations. People need each other, and those needs are the basis for fruitful relations that build positive communities. The liberal model of personality sustains the ideal of a social community in which relations of dependence make mutual assistance mandatory. The self in this vision is not a tough, well-boundaried individualist who must go it alone in life in order to survive and must find within himself all the resources needed; rather, in the liberal vision, the self is fallible, dependent on others, and linked in a variety of ways to other people. Economic life is a web of relations between interdependent people, not the social equivalent of a billiard table with hard balls bouncing off each other. The self is part of a community and cannot be isolated without harm from the relations of trust, care, and help the community affords.

Student Assignment: *My Man Godfrey* (1936)

Made in 1936, just three years after *Gold Diggers*, this film is a conservative response to New Deal liberalism. How is its attitude towards the economic problems of the Great Depression different? How is Godfrey's character different from those in *Gold Diggers*? How is his characterization linked to the film's conservative economic philosophy, which favors entrepreneurship by the wealthy over government action made possible by taxes on the wealthy? How does this film treat morality differently from *Gold Diggers*? Why is self-control an important feature of a conservative economic philosophy? Finally, how is the representational style of this film different? Notice the cut-aways from the crazy family to Godfrey as he calmly observes. How does this style foster a very different feeling about the relationship of individual self to community? Does this film espouse the hard-nosed realism that *Gold Diggers* argues against?

FURTHER READING

Giovacchini, Saverio. *Hollywood Modernism: Film and Politics in the Age of the New Deal*. Philadelphia: Temple University Press, 2001.

Roddick, Rick. *A New Deal in Entertainment: Warner Brothers in the 1930s*. London: British Film Institute, 1983.

Structuralist Criticism

Structuralism was an intellectual movement of the twentieth century that studied culture (and film) using the methods and ideas of linguistics.

The founder of Structuralist Linguistics, Ferdinand de Saussure, described language as a system that is embedded in every utterance we make, much as the rules of chess are embedded in and make possible every move in a game of chess. The language system consists of rules and tools for making utterances. For Saussure, words were signs in which signifiers (sound images) were linked to signifieds (mental images). The crucial idea that Saussure proposed and that would influence later thinkers was that all signs and all parts of language get their identity from their relations to other parts of language. We think our words have identities, which is to say they are completely separate from each other, like closed boxes. Each seems to stand on its own and seems to have its own identity. But words are in fact made up of differences; there are no identities, only relations in language. Words like "rat," "hat," "mat," "cat," etc. exist as separate sounds only as they differ from each other on a sonic continuum, and their identities only exist as an effect of these relations of differences with other terms. Moreover, the alignment of a particular name or word-sound with a particular thing is entirely conventional. We agree there is a match between "rat" and a certain animal, but in reality there could be any number of similar matches that serve the same function. What we call a "rat" could just as easily be called a "hat." There is no necessary link or relation between name and thing. Rather, the relation is conventional, a matter of agreement between users of the language. Words are therefore contingent; they have identities only within certain conventional frameworks upon which they depend to give them meaning. "Rat" means furry quadruped within the frame of the English language, but apart from that, it is a meaningless sound. It has no truth-value in itself.

Language is an artificial system whose connection to the world is arbitrary and conventional. This idea allowed Structuralists to see our cultural sign systems in the same way. We experience the world through systems of cultural signs. Like a language, cultural signs assign an identity to things, much as a word like "hat" assigns a name/identity to something worn on the head. These cultural signs allow us to share certain meanings. For example, we all know what "teacher" and "excellence" refer to. Those terms have meaning within a particular cultural discourse. Like other kinds of language, cultural discourses are conventional and arbitrary; they name things only because agreements allow them to. The signs of cultural discourse have a function within the system of relations and differences of the discourse; but they are not "true" names for things.

Structuralist criticism analyzes how signs function in human culture. Movies consist of signs. The literal actor on screen is a sign that represents a "character" in a fictional story, and that character often represents a particular idea about humanity. Characters in film also enact cultural discourses that are prevalent when the movie is made. For a long time in American movies, for example, Russian characters were signs of danger because the US was engaged in a Cold War with the Soviet Union. The cultural discourse of the Cold War influenced and shaped how people thought and talked during that era. In the dominant representational codes in American film at the time, a positive image of a Russian communist would not have made sense. The dominant meaning was that Russian communists are evil enemies of the US.

Cultural codes are therefore like a norm or unstated rule in that they often tell us what to say and think, and how to behave. When we watch a movie, we see cultural signs that we are meant to read or interpret according to the codes inherent in them. For audiences in the 1950s, for example, the sight of Cary Grant as Roger Thornhill, dressed in a neat, expensive looking blue business suit in the opening segments of *North by Northwest* (1959), would have evoked the idea "respectable businessman." If the filmmakers had chosen to dress him in a black leather jacket and blue jeans, he would, in the sartorial codes of the time, have evoked the much more negative idea "juvenile delinquent." There are of course real hoodlums in the opening segments of *North by Northwest*—the men who kidnap Roger Thornhill. Notice how they are dressed. One wears a casual, sporty looking hat that looks like it belongs on a golf course. The men bear cultural signs, in other words, that place them outside the world of

FIGURE 9.1 *North by Northwest*. The debonair American businessman is portrayed as a hard worker.

"respectable" business that Thornhill inhabits. Their clothes look out of place as much as Thornhill's neat blue suit suggests full agreement with the reigning social norms. It is not a surprise, then, when the men also engage in significant actions—such as pulling out a gun and threatening him in a restaurant—that breach social rules. The audience was able to understand what the film was about and what was going on in it because it used a familiar clothing code (blue business suit versus casual clothes). Because the audience in the 1950s shared with the filmmakers a cultural code of understanding regarding proper dress, they were able to read the film as it was intended.

FIGURE 9.2 *North by Northwest.* The good American is confronted by the bad—and badly dressed—Russian spies.

There are other codes at work in the film. The blue suit Thornhill wears does not only signify "businessman"; it also signifies "world of business" and "America's capitalist economic system, which is run by men like Thornhill." We learn eventually that this is indeed one of the meanings of these initial images. One of the men who kidnaps Thornhill speaks with a slight East European accent, and, at the time the film was made, that would have been a sign of "Russianness." And Russians were, of course, thought by Americans to be enemies of American capitalism in the 1950s and 1960s; they believed in economic equality and opposed the inequality of wealth that accompanies capitalism. In contrast to these men, who steal the luxurious home of a wealthy American to advance their plot against the US, Thornhill is depicted in motion, working as he walks. He represents the idea that American capitalism is dynamic, vital, and industrious. He embodies an ideal of capitalist virtue.

Given the way signs are used in the film's opening sequences, the audience should take away the following thoughts: American business is, like the debonair, well-intentioned Thornhill, a sound and virtuous undertaking that works hard (dictating letters while on the run) and is good at what it does.

Russian socialism, in contrast, like the rude louts who represent it, is violent and unfair; it threatens to harm American business by stealing hard-earned property. While American business plays by the rules, Russian socialism is treacherous. It even, literally and figuratively, stabs people, especially wealthy and successful American businessmen, in the back.

The film, as one might expect, operates within a pro-American code; it takes the side of the US in the Cold War with the Soviet Union that was raging in the 1950s. All the signs at work in the film can be understood within this code. Signs can be anything from style of dress, to speech, to location. There are three significant locations that are worth noting. The first is the Townsend mansion on Long Island. It connotes or signifies wealth, the success of a business career or inherited money from one's family's previous business successes. It is important that this property is taken over by the Russian spies, and especially by a mere gardener, a representative of the working class that Russian socialism favors over the ruling business class. The mansion thus signifies stolen property—what socialism, according to the pro-American code, intends to do with capitalism. The next is the United Nations building. It is important that the true owner of the Townsend property is stabbed in the back by the Russian agent at the UN. The phrase "stab in the back" means to betray, and in the eyes of many Americans, especially those on the pro-business side of the political spectrum in the 1950s, the UN was seen as stabbing America in the back because it often opposed American efforts to stop what it perceived to be an effort on the part of Russian socialists to take over the world and to spread the ideal of economic equality. Finally, Mount Rushmore is significant of American political institutions and ideals such as "rugged individualism" that at the time were offered to the world as alternatives to socialist egalitarianism. That the final events of the film unfold there links the success of Thornhill at thwarting the socialist spies with American institutions. By association, they will also thwart socialism, according to the film.

The film is organized around the idea of treachery and betrayal, and an aspect of signs that the filmmakers underscore constantly is their ability to deceive or to be misunderstood. One cannot trust words or signs; the Russians might say they love peace, but in truth they can be expected to want war. One cannot believe what one hears in a dangerous world characterized by duplicity and betrayal. One should use the weapons of the enemy against him. Liberals favored negotiation, but this conservative film argues that words are false. One would be wiser to rely on deception instead—or to use force.

We get a sense of the treachery of words at the outset of the film when Thornhill dictates letters that make false excuses. He himself is in advertising, a field that stresses false appearances, and he is associated with rhetoric, the use of words to generate effects that may not be true or accurate. He is tricked and trapped by a mere name ("Kaplan") that does not belong to him and that does not signify him. He is a victim of the arbitrariness of signs—that they might signify anything, do not necessarily mean what they seem to signify, and can therefore be used for deception. In the presence of Van Damm, the Russian spy, he continues to assert the truth but is taken for a liar and accused of acting.

Kaplan himself, of course, is a mere sign, a pretense staged by the American CIA to deceive the Russian agents. And Van Damm is himself a pretender, someone who advocates peace at the UN but pursues war by other means behind everyone's backs.

The American intelligence agents are the only ones who know the truth, and the point of the film in part is that Americans should therefore place their trust in them. US intelligence during the Cold War operated largely in secret, and that secrecy was declared to be an expedient necessity, even though it seemed to betray the ideal of democracy and open government that American said it was fighting for. Secrecy was justified in the name of "national security," but it was used to further ends that sometimes had little to do with the nation and more to do with the specific economic interests of US corporations. Military coups aided and abetted by US intelligence in places like Iran, Guatamala, Congo, and Vietnam in the 1950s and 1960s served the interests of American oil, fruit, and mining companies. And sometimes the corporations themselves requested the coups, but little of that was publicly known at the time because of the policy of secrecy this film shows at work and endorses. The film nevertheless alerts us that there must have been a sense in the public's mind that US intelligence was engaged in ruthless, even unethical activities. When the Professor and his US intelligence cohorts first are depicted discussing Thornhill's case, they conclude, somewhat cold-heartedly, that he will have to fend for himself. The higher good takes precedence over mere individuals and mere ethics. The discussion is a reflection of what in political policy discussions of the era was called "realism," the notion that unethical and illegal actions are sometimes needed to counter threats. Perhaps the clearest sign of the need for state secrecy for the sake of the greater good is the sign of silence. When the Professor tells Thornhill at the airport about the mission he, the Professor, is engaged in, an airplane sound blots out what he says so that the audience cannot hear. The film suggests that state secrecy makes popular ignorance necessary for state goals. Those goals include turning the weapon of the enemy against him. The Professor and Thornhill stage Thornhill's death to deceive Van Damm. But US intelligence only makes use of deception. It must present itself as the guardian of truth and of reality. Fittingly, in the end the signifier "reality" is associated with the US intelligence community. After scenes in which a gun with blank cartridges figures prominently, the shooting of the man about to kill Thornhill and Eve Kendall occurs with a real bullet whose reality is commented on in the film.

Student Assignment: *Written on the Wind*

This film is from the same era as *North by Northwest*. How are the signs that appear in this film similar or different from the ones in *Northwest*? The film stages a contrast between two versions of American capitalism, one corporate, the other more small-scale and individualist. What visual signs are associated with each one?

FURTHER READING

Hawkes, Terence. *Structuralism and Semiotics*. Berkeley: University of California Press, 1977.

Scholes, Robert. *Structuralism in Literature*. New Haven: Yale University Press, 1974.

Psychological Criticism

Movies can be studied for psychological meanings in two ways. First, characters are simulated humans with psychological dimensions. Film stories are human life stories; they concern everyday feelings, motives, decisions, and actions. Second, movies are themselves embodiments of psychology. They resemble dreams.

A dream is a series of images that express feelings. You might feel fear over the loss of a girlfriend or boyfriend and dream of being flat on your belly atop a high column that is just three feet wide. The feeling of terror about falling in the dream is a metaphor for the fear of losing your partner.

A movie containing fear images usually also points to feelings. Some are specific to a screenwriter or filmmaker, but some are more general, common, and universal. They are found in all of us. We all fear death, after all, so a movie about zombies eating humans is likely to resonate with all of us.

Most of what is of interest in our psychological lives, Sigmund Freud argued, is unconscious rather than conscious. That is, we are not aware of some our most important feelings, and when they manifest themselves—in dreams, for example—they do so through replacements, substitutes, and displacements. Dreams allow our mind's secret yearnings, fears, and desires to express themselves in conscious form. Freud thought that, in waking life, mental censors guard consciousness and make sure that anxiety-provoking or publicly embarrassing unconscious material does not emerge into public view. At night, the censors go to sleep, and the unconscious begins to express previously repressed feelings in images. Fears and desires that exist in the shadow areas of unconscious life emerge in dreams as full-blown stories with characters and actions and narratives.

Films often operate in the same way. They are fantasies or waking dreams, and they allow unconscious material to be expressed in a substitute form that, unlike the unconscious material itself, possesses structure and coherence. The anxiety-provoking fears and desires that populate the unconscious are given order and meaning in films that make them more presentable and acceptable.

What specific kinds of desire and fear lurk within us in unconscious form? Curiously enough, the two things that most often provoke controversy in film discussions—sex and violence—are also at the heart of our secret psychic lives. We all yearn to form bonds with other people, often if not always in some physical manner. But we also feel hostility, anger, and rage towards others.

169

We are all civilized to the extent that we repress and process these feelings in ways deemed acceptable by our particular societies or cultures. The first major civilizing institution is the family, and much of our unconscious is imprinted with family relations and dynamics. Freud felt that we fashion our personal identities by relating to our parents and even imitating them or adopting them as models. Our first taste of civilized repression comes from learning that we can only yearn for them in mind and not in body. And the frustration of feelings we experience in that family situation can become the motor for all sorts of deviations from what society deems "normal."

This may help explain why so many films worth studying from a psychological perspective have to do with families or with family-like dynamics. We experience our strongest feelings in relation to others, and we are in greatest proximity to others usually in family situations. Frequently, our feelings as adults towards other adults or towards children replicate our own experiences as children. Having been imprinted with an identity by our fathers and mothers, we often act and feel towards those closest to us in ways that reproduce those original relations to our parents. Family films put these processes on display and offer a lesson in the way our psychological identities are formed through relations with others.

There are two major schools of psychology—Freudian psychoanalysis and object relations psychology. Freudianism emphasizes the way unconscious desires and fears emerge in fantasies like films. Object relations theory places much less emphasis on the unconscious and focuses instead on relations between people. According to object relations theory, our inner selves are shaped by the relations we have as children with our caregivers. We internalize images of caregivers, and those internalizations or mental representations permit us to separate from them and to become independent subjects. Initially, we are fused to caregivers and to the world of objects and have difficulty demarcating ourselves as subjects from the object world around us. But with the aid of internalizations—mental representation we construct in our minds of others to whom we relate—we are able to build up our own sense of a separate identity. We learn to separate from that initial fusion and to take the world as a separate object of cognition. By learning to make mental images of objects such as a mother or a father, we in effect posit them as being separate from ourselves and end our early fusion with them. By attaining object constancy—a sense of a stable and continuously perceived world "out there"—we also attain a separate self-identity. A crucial issue in object relations psychology, therefore, is the question of the success or failure of this process of separation and identity-building. And crucial to that issue is the question of boundaries between ourselves and our objects (other people). We acquire a separate individual identity by acquiring the capacity to establish boundaries between ourselves and the world or between ourselves and others. Psychopathology in this account takes the form of either an excessive yearning for separation or an excessive need for fusion with others, either too feeble a sense of self-identity or too exaggerated a sense of boundaries. For example, in *The Birds*, Mitch, who begins as excessively welded to his mother, eventually learns to separate, and this is figured in his labors to seal the boundaries of the house. He is metaphorically restoring personal boundaries that his mother had inappropriately overwhelmed by bonding too closely with him after her husband's death.

The psychoanalytic study of film assumes that films are like dreams—they both reveal the unconscious and conceal it behind images that seem to have nothing to do with it. They also displace central psychological concerns into illogically marginal places that make them seem of less importance than in fact they are. These are the ego defenses at work, policing the boundary between the hidden parts of our psyches and the conscious and self-aware parts, making sure that material that is dangerous for the ego because it is embarrassing or upsetting does not make it through into expression unless it is toned down and made safe. Those defenses displace anxiety-provoking material away from its cause and move it to a place (in a dream or in a film) that make it appear of less importance. They also turn feelings into their opposites, so that a yearning for a forbidden object becomes a desire to push that object away.

The story of *The Silence of the Lambs* concerns the control that consciousness affords and the uncontrollable desires that reside in the unconscious. The four primary characters—Clarice Starling, Jamie Gumm, Hannibal Lecter, and John Crawford—can all be situated in relation to this core concern or problem.

Hannibal Lecter, the insane criminal, is a reasonable man who is simultaneously unreasonable. He inhabits mind and body; thinks reasonably yet indulges bodily urges of the most physical of kinds. He is highly civilized, yet he represents the deepest possible breach of civility. Instead of behaving with civil distance toward others, he devours them, removing all distance, civil as well as physical.

FIGURE 10.1 *The Silence of the Lambs.* Hannibal Lecter is portrayed as simultaneously rational and irrational.

Clarice Starling, the young FBI agent, is similarly mixed. She progresses from a neophyte who inhabits both mind and body, the emotional and the rational, to a position of power and achievement associated with the mind, reason, consciousness. She successfully represses the bodily, unconscious urges that subvert reason. Clarice becomes in the end a model of rational clarification.

She is helped by John Crawford, the embodiment of professional control and reason. He is associated with mental strategies that bring order to the disorderly material and resolution to the confusion bred by unconscious impulses that have been allowed to get out of control and to attain expression.

Finally, Jamie Gumm represents the unconscious material against which the rational mind works. He lives underground, in a symbolic space opposed to the symbolically upper-storey rational operations lodged in FBI headquarters, and he is the embodiment of the confusion that results when primary physical urges are not restrained. Like Lecter, he consumes others' bodies, but, unlike Lecter, he has no way of rationally rising above the confusion of identity the unleashing of the unconscious brings about.

What is the source of the confusion in Jamie's life? What provokes uncertainty regarding gender identity in a boy? One source is a prolonged attachment to the mother. That attachment prevents the boy from gaining the boundaries that would separate his identity from his mother's and his body from hers. The dissolving of boundaries is often associated with liquid, and it is extremely important that Jamie's underground world contains a bathtub in which the body of the previous owner of his house, the maternal Mrs. Lipman, has mouldered away into a mush. Her body is a symbol of the problem he himself lives out and represents—the dissolution of "proper" gender boundaries that would establish him as a male. Instead, he longs to be a female. The image of the dead woman's body appears in a marginal moment of the film, when Clarice is searching for Jamie, but it is one of those significant displacements of important psychic material into a scarcely noticeable corner that psychoanalysts notice. Her centrality is indicated, if you will, by her ostentatious lack of centrality. The thing that would reveal to a psychoanalyst like Lecter what Jamie's real problem is—an "excessive" attachment to his mother—is instead pushed to the side in the hope that it might not be noticed.

Clarice's progress in the film consists of putting aside emotion, weakness, and lack of rational control over her body's feelings in order to achieve a professional identity associated with reason, strength of mind, and self-control. Her progress is overseen by two "fathers" or guides—Crawford and Lecter— and both of them are characterized as possessing powerful minds or as embodiments of self-control. If the two fathers work logically to establish the identity of Jamie Gumm, he in turn represents the subversion of proper identities, the mixture of distinct elements that confuses reason and eludes control. If reason operates by assuming a norm that then makes the control of deviations from the norm necessary, Jamie has no sense of that distinction and operates in a realm of mixture that confounds the difference between norm and deviation. If the heterosexual norm arises out of a sense of identity that supposedly expresses an existing nature, Jamie cuts and stitches to make a nature of his own, thus reversing the proper order of identity. His identity does not derive from nature; rather, he manufactures an identity by rearranging nature. He is an emblem of pure deviation and change, and his symbol in the film, fittingly, is the pupa that molts into a butterfly or moth.

Jamie works, literally, on bodies, cutting and sewing to create his new female identity. He has not learned to repress his urges, to be in control and to act reasonably. He would need, of course, to become a heterosexual male or to identify with the dominant heterosexual male culture to attain this end. Lecter, in contrast, urges Clarice to adhere to first principles and to see what things are in themselves. "What is its nature?" he tells her to ask of Jamie. Things in themselves have boundaries, distinct natures, and identities of their own. Jamie represents a threat to this ideal of rational social as well as personal order.

As Clarice at the outset runs through the FBI training course, she passes a sign that speaks of hurt, agony, and pain, and concludes "love it." The FBI's exercise of scientific reason against the irrational threat to both legal and rational order is thus coded as the power to make the body submit. Later, she and her friend Ardelia are portrayed memorizing FBI rules. By the end, she will have achieved a professional identity molded on the model of Crawford. Small editing details describe her progress, as when Catherine is kidnapped violently by Jamie, who clubs her with a fake cast over his arm. The film cuts from this scene to an image of Clarice in training fending off blows from another male FBI student. Her ability to maintain her bodily boundaries suggests an antidote to Jamie, who connotes a breakdown of boundaries.

A hint of Lecter's role in helping her transcend the body and to learn to be more rational and in control is given when he sniffs in the initial prison hospital encounter and says he cannot smell her genitals. He exists on the boundary between body and mind, reason and unreason, and he helps her sort out the mucky bodily messes that Jamie leaves in his wake on his quest to identify with femininity. Both Jamie and Lecter are positioned in underground spaces, a topographical metaphor for the body "below." Jamie is incapable of transcending this positioning and indeed revels in it (the place where he keeps his liquefied mother figure and where he plays with women's bodies and with his own). Lecter's powerful mind allows him to escape his dungeon, to kill Meigs, and to conquer that other subverter of rational rules by inappropriate emotional and bodily urges—Dr. Chilton. While Lecter, like Crawford, is linked to the rules of courtesy and reason that maintain boundaries and that aid Clarice's transcendence of the body in favor of the mind, Chilton makes a pass at her and reduces her to bodily life. He thus more resembles Meigs in the film's structuring of characters than Lecter or Crawford. He lacks civil restraint. Fittingly, at the end of the narrative, he is symbolically expunged.

The more important parallel for Lecter, from Clarice's perspective, is Crawford, her teacher and mentor in the FBI. When she says "I don't know how to feel about this," his reply is instructive: "You don't have to feel anything." He represents the possibility that she might learn the rules, become more rational, scientific, and in control, and acquire a professional identity that allows her to master the confusion associated with Jamie and with emotions in general.

Lecter represents a similar possibility of learning reason, but he instructs her to be aware of emotions that might link her to Jamie's wayward impulses. When she discovers the head of Jamie's first victim, it is after having followed Lecter's instruction to "look inside yourself." The word "yourself" has a double meaning. It refers to a storage locker, but it also refers to Clarice. She wants to be "like her father," a policeman, and that desire differentiates her from Jamie who wants to be like his mother. After Clarice finds the head, Lecter asks her: "How did it feel?" And her response—that she was at first scared, then "exhilarated"—associates her with Lecter and Jamie's propensity to take pleasure in another's pain or death. By looking inside herself, she can find a version of Jamie, someone with emotions, a body, potentially irrational urges or feelings, and a yearning to cross-dress and to identify with someone of the opposite gender. If he wishes to be a woman, she wishes to be a man, or at least someone who conforms to the ideals of reason associated with men in the movie.

But unlike Lecter or Jamie, who remain connected to bodily urges and to bodies through their perverse and irrational labors and preferences, Clarice has Crawford and the FBI to lift her out of the bodily realm of feeling and violence and to elevate her above the body and all that it connotes of emotionality, irrationality, and uncontrollability. If Lecter makes Clarice look at her emotions and learn to control them, Crawford makes her look literally at bodies. In the examination scene, he instructs her on how to describe the dead woman's body that was taken from a river. This rational distancing of the literal body (figured in the taking of photographs—a metaphor for mental representations that distance the growing child from its mother by allowing him/her to take the mother's body as an object pictured in mental images) is linked to a parallel training in the management of men from her own class background. At the examination of the murder victim, Crawford tells the police chief, who is about to get angry, that they should speak in private because Clarice is present. This ruse controls the man's anger and manages him. Similarly, shortly thereafter, Clarice tells the roomful of policemen to leave by playing to their feelings of courtesy and flattering them. Later, she will join Crawford in managing Lecter by making him a false offer of a different kind of prison.

What she is conquering in Jamie is a tendency to be literally attached to bodily life and to fail to perform the rational procedure of distancing bodily life with what object relations psychologists call mental representations. Jamie is someone who fails to transcend the literality of the body by creating mental images that distance him from physicality, especially the physicality of the mother's body. It is this failure that gives rise to confusion—of conscious and unconscious processes and of gender identity. In contrast, Clarice learns from Lecter how higher-order rational symbols are made, ones that replace literal objects with mental representations. He speaks in riddles whose meaning she must learn to unravel and interpret. Jamie, he tells her, is like a moth that wants to change. That is the significance of the literal moth Jamie has placed in one of his victims, a moth which Clarice discovers. And "moth" of course links the murder literally to the "moth-er" to whom Jamie is dangerously, irrationally, excessively attached. If Jamie is too literal, too attached to bodies, emotions,

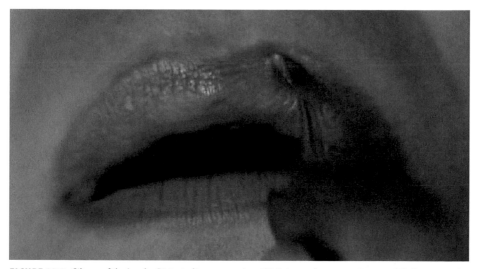

FIGURE 10.2 *Silence of the Lambs.* Distorted images such as this intense close-up portray negatively a man who longs to become a woman.

and, by implication, irrationality, Clarice, to conquer what he represents, must conquer those very qualities in herself and learn to be rational, symbolic, and metaphoric. These processes will give her control over the body and over her emotions.

Lecter instructs Clarice regarding the metaphoric character of her own motives. Her desire to save Catherine is really a desire to silence the lambs she heard crying as a child. By making such logical as well as metaphoric connections and by seeing how images substitute metaphorically for things, objects, and bodies, she learns to rise above bodily motives and bodily urges. She moves beyond emotion and learns to reason, to replace literal things with figurative signs. The posture of holding a gun and shooting at things had earlier had the meaning of an antidote to her emotional vulnerability. It returns at the end in Jamie's basement, a fitting metaphor for her conquest of her own demons and her own unconscious. With Catherine screaming from a well, a metaphor for the body out of control, Clarice manages the situation by calming Catherine and undoing her earlier mistake of not watching her blind side in a training exercise. She successfully shoots Jamie, an act that also metaphorically opens windows that shed light on darkness and brings clarity to gender confusion. What she has killed off in Jamie is the confusion and mixture that the release of unconscious urges provokes, a mixture embodied in the motley rug covering his body.

But in another reading, what Jamie represents is the possibility that the dominant gender norm represses other natural urges than the heterosexual one. The transformation of one among many sex/gender preferences into a rational-seeming norm does violence to the natural plurality of sex/gender proclivities. The real serial killers in the film, from this perspective, are Crawford and Clarice, the emblems of a repressive sex/gender regime that maintains its only apparent rationality and normativity by regularly and systematically doing violence to the alternatives. The curious thing about the film, of course, is that it really is about a successful sex change operation. Clarice does, in essence, become a professional man, or, at least, the image of a professional man. In a society dominated by heterosexual male imperatives, people of either gender seem to have little choice, if this film is to be believed, beyond identifying in one way or another with the father.

Student Assignment: *Revolutionary Road* (2008)

This film explores psychological identities that many ascribe to a particular period in American history—the 1950s. It was a time when conservative ideals and values dominated public discourse. America supposedly turned inward; men became more conformist; and women became housewives and gave up hopes of being workers or professionals. The psychological and emotional costs were extreme. How does this film depict those costs? To what degree are the characters' psychological plights due to their own temperaments or to their familial and work environments? What role does the "mad" character play in the story? What does he represent?

FURTHER READING

Cooper, Arnold. *Contemporary Psychoanalysis in America*. Washington: American Psychiatric Publishers, 2006.

de Berg, Henk. *Freud's Theory and its Use in Literary and Cultural Studies*. Woodbridge: Camden House, 2003.

Freud, Sigmund. *The Interpretation of Dreams*. Oxford: Oxford University Press, 1999.

Gordon, Paul. *Dial 'M' for Mother: A Freudian Hitchcock*. Madison: Farleigh Dickinson University Press, 2008.

Understanding the Dream World: Moving Beyond Freud. New York: Films Media Group, 2006.

Ideological Criticism

Most movies you are likely to see are made in capitalist societies, and, in such societies, those with a great deal of wealth usually own and control the means of producing more wealth—factories, corporations, businesses, and the like. Those without much inherited wealth tend to have to work for the first group. If the first group owns, the second group labors. They depend on each other in a modern capitalist system, but the first group has the upper hand economically and, by implication, politically.

Why is this important for understanding movies?

If the owning group do not control the political institutions directly, they exercise a great deal of influence over society by virtue of owning and controlling the means of distributing ideas in the society. They own the media, and they produce movies. Rupert Murdoch owns and controls large parts of the media around the world, including Fox News, and, as a wealthy conservative, the ideas his companies promote tend to reinforce the power of wealthy men like him. They make the unequal distribution of wealth seem the result of "freedom" and they portray efforts to bring about a more fair distribution of wealth by government policy as irrational and dangerous.

The ideas that are dominant in human societies tend to cohere with the practices and institutions of the society, and they usually work to solidify and reinforce, rather than challenge, the distribution of resources and power in the society. An obvious example of this would be the idea that nobles are naturally superior to commoners, an idea that helped sustain an unequal class structure in medieval Europe for many centuries. Those who believed the idea were likely to behave in certain ways that allowed that structure to reproduce itself from generation to generation.

The dominant idea in modern capitalist economies is "freedom." Such economies tend on the whole to distribute rewards unequally, and many critics of capitalism argue that the ideal of freedom works to sustain such inequality. It means that people who are chained to a life of labor that ultimately benefits others more than themselves believe that they are free when in fact they are dominated and exploited. Ideology names the way ideas secure the domination of one class over another in capitalist societies by making inequality seem justified and by making those who are allocated fewer resources feel comfortable with their comparative deprivation. According to this theory of culture, the idea of "freedom" is dominant in the United States not because everyone actually is free but because that idea reinforces the power of the wealthy and the business class (who exercise a great say in what counts as legitimate ideas in the culture). Under the banner of freedom, those groups can use their economic power to gain more wealth and power for themselves. They are "free" to do so. The ideal of freedom also assures that those they exploit will not use the one instrument at their disposal—the government—to restrain the power of the economic elite. The use of government power to redistribute wealth in a more egalitarian manner would be an offense to freedom. By making the ideal of freedom paramount in society, those who rule economically can convince those they exploit that their lesser position in society is deserved and even desirable. They too are free to strive to "get ahead," even though they more often than not stay in the economic class in which they were born. The capitalist ideology of freedom is most effective when it makes the ideal of individual mobility cohere with a reality of stagnant structural social inequality. Two things that would be entirely incompatible if considered logically are thus made compatible by virtue of a kind of thinking that eschews logic in favor of a more emotive kind of reasoning. Chains are made to seem a pleasing part of one's wardrobe.

Consider *Working Girl* (1988), a film about a young woman, Tess McGill, who works as a secretary in New York and takes night classes in Business and proper English in order to better her station. Through a convoluted plot, she succeeds in getting in the end a much better job in a corporation, one far above the station she seemed to be assigned at the beginning of the film. In order to understand why this positive upbeat narrative might be an example of ideology, one must be aware that during this time period—from the late 1970s through the 1990s in the US—income differentiation between the top fifth and bottom fifth increased dramatically. While the booming economy of the last part of this era benefited the top fifth enormously, the income of the bottom fifth declined. Most of the Tess McGills of this world were going nowhere fast. Many, at the time the film was made, were being fired as a result of corporate downsizing for the sake of greater efficiency and profitability to benefit wealthy investors. Many were ending up in service sector jobs—cleaning houses, cutting hair, serving food, etc. Formerly middle-class Americans, in other words, were being pushed into menial, low-income lives with little future chance of significant changes in income or status.

Why would so painful a reality be represented altogether differently in a major film of the era, one that takes suffering and anguish and transforms it into a chipper, feel-good evocation of hope, success, and self-transformation? It seems an unwritten rule of societies founded on radical inequalities of wealth and station that the culture not represent accurately those inequalities; otherwise the culture, instead of assuring a commonality of feeling that would hold the society together, might foster resentment, demands for change, and quite possibly revolution. Films are most ideological when, in the face of extremes of deprivation and potential anger, they foster false hope and futile aspiration, as well as a feeling that the society's institutions, regardless of what inequalities they produce, are just and right. *Working Girl* is a very good example of this.

Here is the story of the film: Tess's boss Catherine is a wealthy, well-educated, and successful businesswoman. But when Tess brings to Catherine an idea of her own regarding the acquisition of radio stations by Trask Enterprises, one of Catherine's clients, Catherine steals it and pretends it's her own. When Catherine is laid up in Europe for two weeks after a skiing accident, Tess discovers her treachery and decides to pretend to be an investment banker instead of a secretary in order to pursue her idea herself. She takes on Catherine's identity, dresses up like her, learns to speak like her, and goes to meetings in her place. She accidentally manages to steal Catherine's boyfriend, Jack Trainor, away from her, and he, a merger specialist, helps her to succeed with her idea. Catherine returns suddenly during the meeting at which Tess, Jack, and Trask are about to finalize the deal, discloses Tess's duplicity, and reveals to Trask and Jack that Tess is actually only a secretary pretending to be something and someone she isn't. She also claims the idea for the acquisition was her own, not Tess's. Tess seems defeated, but she finds a way of proving to Trask that the idea was actually her own and that Catherine is lying. Catherine is defeated, Tess gets a job at Trask Enterprises, and she and Jack, both dressed for business, are in the end shown living happily together and getting ready to go off to work.

It's important to note the class vocabulary of the film. Tess initially has "big hair," a puffed hairstyle common among young working-class women in the 1980s. Once she becomes Catherine, she cuts her hair and assumes a more corporate look. Initially, she is depicted living in a working-class neighborhood across the river from Manhattan, where Catherine presumably lives and where their corporation is located. Once she assumes Catherine's identity, she moves into Catherine's upscale apartment. Tess's boyfriend is from the working class, and she leaves him for Jack, who, like Catherine, is a successful businessperson. Her trajectory is therefore upward in several measurable ways.

What could be wrong with this success story that in some respects seems so typically "American," in that the country is supposedly founded on an ideal of freedom that allows for untrammeled mobility both socially and economically?

Let's consider some ways in which it might be read or interpreted as being ideological, as reinforcing inequality even as it appears to transcend it, at least in this individual case. If one compares Tess's story to the actual or real stories of the thousands of young women like her, her success is remarkable and atypical. Indeed, the filmmakers must evoke that atypicality in order to underscore her unique virtue. They do this by twinning her with a friend who lacks Tess's desire to rise above her station and by locating her initially within a mass of other women like herself from whom she must successfully separate and differentiate herself. When Tess finally gets what she wants—an upper level, non-secretarial corporate job—the achievement is depicted through a contrast edit which moves from a shot of Tess alone in her new office to a shot of her friend back in a large secretarial office crowded with other secretaries. Tess's individual success is presented as being atypical, a departure from the norm for young women like herself, at the very moment that the film offers her to the audience as an object of universal identification, as someone with whose trajectory of individual success a mass of people might identify. The film argues that anyone with spunk and ingenuity can rise in the business world, but, in order to do this, it must simultaneously aver through the necessary contrast edit that underscores her individual and uncommon achievement that very few can or will actually do so. A certain Horatio Algerism common in American culture, the belief that individual initiative in anyone can produce wealth, crosses with a certain Social Darwinism which is equally powerful in American culture, the belief that only the fit survive and rise to the top of the income ladder, leaving the less able or less motivated behind. In order to measure Tess's achievement, the film must use a baseline of the larger unmoving female secretarial pool that must be depicted as stuck in its place. If they all could be Tesses, there would be no Tesses, nor would there be an American economy as we know it, since there would be no one at the bottom to do the drudge labor that gives others the free time to do the more lucrative upper-level jobs. At the very moment when the film would seem to celebrate the democratic openness of the American economic system, it depicts it as a closed trap from which very few on the bottom will escape because, if they did, it would ruin the system.

The film privileges the positive redemptive side of that contradiction. The other secretaries are in the background, Tess the foreground. Her story of individual success is at the center of the narrative, and that tipping toward the positive of the contradiction between her individual case and the numerous very different cases unlike her own is what ideology is all about. It doesn't deny reality; it simply allows social reality to be interpreted in such a way that it will remain the same and seem unworthy of being challenged. The negative side of the contradiction will simply be read as justifying the positive side. Tess's story of upward mobility may require an immobile background of many lives unlike her own, but her story offers hope to anyone stuck in that background. That may not be a very logical way to think, but ideology works precisely by urging us toward alogical conclusions based on evidence that would more logically lead to very different ideas.

Furthermore, the film is ideological in the way that it implicitly endorses the hierarchical structure of modern economic life. Almost all films endorse the world they represent, of course, but that endorsement shifts toward ideology when it is applied to regimes of inequality in which one group's participation is predicated on their acceptance of fewer gains than the dominant group, especially if they do much of the labor that produces those gains. That, at least, is one reading of modern capitalism: many people work producing wealth so that a few can enjoy the benefits through an inequitable distribution of the resulting profits. The film is ideological in that Tess's great idea is one that will allow a single man—Trask—to greatly increase his wealth. Her self-annulment in favor of his gain is her greatest achievement in the film.

The film takes the structural inequality between his status as owner and her status as worker devoted to increasing his wealth for granted. That difference in power becomes at one point a key mover in the plot of the film. Tess is packing up her office after having been exposed as a secretary before Trask and expelled from the meeting negotiating the acquisition she has devised. Trask, Catherine, and Jack walk into the office building, and in the encounter that follows, Tess

FIGURES 11.1 & 11.2 *Working Girl*. The heroine can win only by leaving her fellow secretaries behind, and they must remain stuck where they are if her rise to an office of her own is to have the meaning of an accomplishment.

convinces Trask that she—not Catherine—came up with the important idea. He then confronts Catherine and tells her she will lose her job. The plot, in other words, could not proceed without his power and his authority over others. Like capitalism itself, the plot seems to work for Tess's benefit, but in fact it works for his benefit. Its crucial hinge presupposes and reassures his power, his ability to proffer patronage, thus augmenting his symbolic wealth as patron of the poor in the eyes of the audience, even as it "saves" Tess and lifts her up. The labor of plot resolution will secure her a place in his office building, placing her under him in her work in much the same way that it must situate her under him for the narrative resolution to be effectuated. The story of her great success thus presupposes and reinforces an inequality of power that dictates that her upward mobility has a limit somewhere around his feet. From that point, she can look down at her friend and be grateful she's no longer stuck with the mass of secretaries, but she will always also have to look up to the further rungs where the Trasks of the world live, forever beyond her reach if she continues to define her identity, her virtue, and her trajectory in life in terms of the augmentation of their wealth and power. She merely pushes them further away up the ladder as she climbs up behind. On this particular ladder of success, they rest comfortably on her head.

In watching the film and appreciating uncritically its story, we must endorse and celebrate inequality as much as individual success. We must give assent to a social system that designates certain people as less worthy than others, and we must accede to a regime of social power that allocates resources in such a way that a small minority (a single man in the case of this film) will benefit enormously from the labors of numerous others. A film is most successfully ideological when it gets us to do these things without realizing we are doing so. It gets us to see the world one way but to interpret in another. We see structural inequality but interpret it as individual success. To do so, we must know but never think that Tess will never be Trask, that her destiny is given in the final image of the film—rows of windows all alike, one of which is hers—which suggests that she is multiple, that her seemingly differentiated individuality is multiply replicated in a mass of lives very much like her own, laboring away for the only real individual in the film, the only real individual success story, the man who owns and who, by owning, rules. Tess rebels against her old life in order to be respectfully obedient in her new one. That apparently is all that the system allows.

Student Assignment: *Die Hard* (1988)

Die Hard is about a working-class "stiff" who defends corporate America. John belongs to a group called "Reagan Democrats" who had enormous political influence in the US in the eighties and nineties. Working-class white men traditionally voted for Democrats but began in the late 1960s to vote for conservative Republicans as they grew disenchanted with liberal support for Civil Rights, for opposition to the war in Vietnam, and for social rights such as the right to abortion. These men valued toughness on a personal and a national level. As the economy declined in the 1970s and their incomes stagnated, they believed Republicans who blamed "big government" taxation for the hardships faced by the middle class, and they opposed programs such as affirmative action that sought to rectify past discrimination against African-Americans and other ethnic minorities by giving them job preference. They were cultural fundamentalists who believed a woman's place was in the home, kids should obey their fathers, and social authority should be respected.

How does John embody the values and ideals of the Reagan Democrats?

How is "big government" portrayed in this film? Government is often associated by conservatives with irrational bureaucratic rules and uniformity.

The ideal of individual freedom is narcissistic. That is, rather than think of one's responsibility towards the community one lives in, one thinks of oneself and privileges one's own needs and desires over responsibility to or for others. How is the portrait of John narcissistic? Think of how Al is portrayed as a buddy who "roots" for him. Note also images of reflection, wounding, and acclaim. One possible way working-class men might secure a modicum of self-esteem for themselves in a world that denies them the usual external signs of worth such as wealth is to think of themselves as secret heroes whose worth is not recognized by society. How does this structure of self-esteem appear in John's characterization?

FURTHER READING

Bailey, Gordon. *Ideology: Structuring Identities in Contemporary Life*. New York: Broadview, 2003.

Dumont, Louis. *Essays on Individualism: Modern Ideology in Anthropological Perspective*. Chicago: University of Chicago Press, 1986.

Levine, Andrew. *The American Ideology*. London: Routledge, 2004.

McLellan, David. *Ideology*. Minneapolis: University of Minnesota Press, 1995.

Marietta, Morgan. *A Citizen's Guide to American Ideology*. New York: Routledge, 2012.

Gender Criticism

Film provides a remarkable cultural history of gender. Whenever we tell imaginary stories in film, we record our assumptions regarding a host of social institutions, and gender is one of the most interesting of these institutions because it has changed so much during the film era over the course of the last century or so.

Feminist film scholars were the first to notice that women in films were often portrayed in ways that helped to solidify or reinforce their subordinate position in society. The images in film portrayed as virtuous women who knew their place in the social hierarchy and depicted as vicious women who manifested too many signs of independence or personal strength. Such scholars challenged the idea that gender as it appears in film culture is a reflection of nature. They pointed out that women can be as masculine as men, while many men have more feminine temperaments. Despite being biologically female, masculine women may like feminine men or feminine women or mixtures of each. Yet films have consistently argued that men are masculine and women feminine and that masculine women are evil and feminine men are somehow lesser beings. The contingency or accidental character of the link between gender and biology meant that consistent training and indoctrination were required to assure that the appearance of a natural link between gender and biology was maintained. In film, men had to be (reminded that they were) masculine men, and women (reminded that they were) feminine women if men were to be men and women women in society—that is, if "man" and "woman" were to mean strong and independent on the one hand and weak and dependent on the other. A certain amount of coercive, disciplinary cultural force was required to make sure "nature" was what many believed it should be.

Gender is shaped by cultural ideal, but it is often at odds with biological reality. If women experience a conflict between their own powers and capacities on the one hand and the subordinate position male-dominated society has traditionally allocated them, men experience a contradiction between the manly virtues such as inner strength, independence, resourcefulness, and toughness required to occupy the dominant social position they are allocated in male-dominated society on the one hand and the vulnerable, relational make-up of their actual gender identity on the other. In reality, they are anything but independent, self-reliant, and self-contained, just as in reality women are not weak, dependent, and passive. No one is self-contained in a culture in which one's identity is assigned and, in being assigned, constituted through relational differences from other shades of identity. The great task of cultural gendering is to try to make the manufacture of gender identity, through the conversion of relations and differentiations into seemingly self-contained wholes, boxes without windows, appear to be the reflection or expression of a natural process, one with a firm foundation in ontology or natural being. The factory must appear to be a mine.

Let's consider a film from a particularly vexed moment in American gender history—near the end of World War II—when it was becoming clear that there would be a clash for jobs between the men who had been away and the women who had stayed home to "man" the factories. Released in 1944, *Mildred Pierce* is the story of a woman who leaves her husband and sets out to become an economic success by opening a chain of restaurants. Her daughter, Veda, murders Mildred's second husband, Monty, at the outset of the film, and the detective story follows the investigation that leads to the discovery of the murderer, but that story overlaps with the story of Mildred's post-marriage life. The police detective makes clear the link between the two narrative strands when he asks of Mildred's first husband, "Well if he's so wonderful, Mrs. Beragon, why then did you divorce him?" It's an odd question for a detective to pose, but it makes sense in a film whose ultimate thematic purpose is to portray Mildred as having made a mistake. She divorced and sought an independent economic life. The film is as much the investigation of a divorce as of a murder. Made near the end of World War II, the film can be seen as part of an effort in America to convince women to return to the home and to take up more domestic, traditionally feminine roles and identities.

In response to the detective's question, Mildred begins her first flashback and tells of her life with Bert and her two kids, Veda and Kay. The film cuts from the dark of the detective's office to a well-lit, sunny street that emanates material comfort and is alive with the joys of childhood and family life. That very positive image is at odds with the slightly complaining description of her life offered by Mildred in the voiceover: "Sometimes I thought I spent my whole life in a kitchen. I never knew any other kind of life—just cooking and washing and having children." A similar conflict between visual and aural messages occurs when Bert returns home to announce he has no job. He stands under a gothic arch that endows him with religious significance, a foreshadowing of the end of the film, when Bert and Mildred reunite and march off together to the sound of church bells chiming under a similar arch. Yet the dialog at this point suggests that it is Mildred who is getting the bad end of the bargain: Bert has a mistress, Maggie Biederhof, who telephones while he and Mildred argue over the children and his lack of a job.

By this point, the detective's question has been answered in Mildred's favor: Bert is disloyal, and that is one reason she divorces him. But the film is not going to be tilted in her favor, and the central issue of that larger argument emerges in the accusation Bert levels at her of spoiling their daughter, Veda.

Indeed, their break occurs when he, like a good old-fashioned patriarch, threatens to hit or discipline Veda for talking back. The crucial conflict at this point is between maternal indulgence and paternal discipline, and the destructive effects of maternal indulgence on the film world's moral values will not become clear until much later. By the end of the film we will know that Bert was right and Mildred wrong. Had she been properly disciplined, Veda would not have turned out to be a murderer—or, at least, so the film asserts.

Discipline is not the only source of conflict regarding Veda. Veda's yearning for material possessions and for class mobility also opens a gap between father and mother, with Mildred wishing to give Veda everything she herself was denied in life, including expensive singing lessons, and Bert arguing that money should not be wasted on "spoiling" kids with material things. The film portrays virtue as an inner trait that exists apart from material possessions. Bert has it and is unconcerned about material advancement. Veda does not and is consumed with material desires. Mildred sides with Veda and gives up her life of virtuous self-sacrifice in the family kitchen to become a businesswoman so that she can satisfy Veda's exorbitant material yearnings.

The film's gender values are especially pronounced in the way Veda is characterized. She is depicted as nothing short of a monster who ultimately betrays her own mother by sleeping with her new step-father. In the absence of a firm paternal disciplinary hand to keep boundaries straight, children, the film suggests, confuse right and wrong, and it reserves its most audaciously black visual compositions for the moment when incest is discovered in the basement of the beach house. Blurred visual boundaries become a metaphor for erased moral boundaries.

Yet in considering the film from a gender perspective, we should ask why a woman who yearns for escape from poverty and longs to move up the class ladder is portrayed as a monster. Were she a man, her ambitions would be characterized as the worthy motives for the dynamic actions of an energetic go-getter. But as a woman, at this time in history at least, when America was getting ready to send women back to the home to tend to all those returning veterans and to vacate jobs for those men to occupy, she could only be portrayed positively if she accepted limits that she is not willing to accept. Mildred is willing, of course, and that is what redeems her in the end. As she walks out with Bert to the sound of church bells, two women kneel on the floor scrubbing, an image that seems intended as an ideal for Mildred now to follow.

Because the film rests on gender assumptions that assign independence and strength to men and an ideal of domestic service to women, all the women who break the domestic mold are portrayed as being mannish. Joan Crawford's costumes in the film are famous for their broad shoulders. Having crossed the line separating home from work, she has apparently crossed a gender divide as well. It is significant that her best friend in the business world, Ida, is portrayed as something of a masculine or butch lesbian, although the anti-gay cultural codes of the time required that she be presented as interested in men

FIGURE 12.1 *Mildred Pierce.* In the final image, a woman is restored to a more traditional identity.

and frustrated by their lack of attention. At the moment of Mildred's greatest separation from and disenchantment with men, her friendship with Ida is at its strongest. Fittingly, during the police processing that seems destined to restore not only moral order but gender order as well, Mildred and Ida are enjoined from talking to each other. Women's communication amongst themselves, which for Ida and Mildred meant banter critical of men, seems aligned on a spectrum that also includes acts against the reigning moral order. It is as if women who become masculine or women who withdraw from the world of men into a world of their own are dangerous in some way to the patricentric values the film endorses.

The hint of lesbian possibilities in Ida's characterization is echoed in the way the relationship between Mildred and Veda is portrayed. In a structural or psychoanalytic sense, Veda has to be seen as a projection of Mildred's own fantasies and yearnings. Everything she has been denied will be Veda's. That psychological mirroring becomes a kind of physical enfolding when Veda at the end accuses Mildred of being responsible for how she is. Veda nuzzles against Mildred, and Mildred's open mouth suggests an erotic charge. Moral culpability crosses with physical proximity; the mother's fault is too proximate an emotional and physical relation to her daughter. She is her daughter in some respects. They have not successfully separated. The father has not intervened to establish proper boundaries between them, boundaries that are also the

FIGURE 12.2 *Mildred Pierce*. The relation of a mother and her daughter is given an erotic inflection.

boundaries of moral propriety. The erotic character of the relation has already been suggested in the bedroom scene, when Mildred, after having kicked the husband and father out of the house, takes advantage of the dropping of the moral imperatives embodied and instantiated in the father's patriarchal authority in the domestic scene by leaning over Veda to kiss her good-night—exactly the kind of indulgence the husband/father counseled against. Veda tells her not to be too sticky, an erotically charged word that echoes Mildred's own word to Wally when he leaned over her and tried to kiss her. What is sticky is both erotic and without boundaries, a fluid that lacks the walls of solid objects. Mildred and Veda's world is similarly fluid, lacking in properly separated identities.

The restoration of patriarchal order is metaphorized appropriately as doorways and windows, things whose openness between realms underscores the presence of walls and other lines of demarcation. The detective walks to the window, opens the shade, and sheds light on Mildred's dark world of duplicity and double identity. Bert walks her out through a doorway into the morning light. Veda is framed in the light of a door, a white box that finally cages in her wayward will. Shadow and darkness pertains to the world of women, according to the men making the movie. Men are portrayed in the film as the guardians of a logical, rational moral and social order predicated on clear enlightened knowledge. Women fold in on themselves, psychological equivalents of the sexual world harbored in the secret, out-of-view place between their legs. Women's danger in the film is thus figured as Wally's entrapment in an inwardly spiraling stairway chamber. They lead men astray, prevent clear knowledge, block the light of reason in the folds of duplicitous emotion and self-doubling bonds which exclude men.

The form of the film most embodies this meaning in the opening sequence, when an illogical edit moves from the murder to a woman walking mysteriously along a pier. If this were a film about male concerns rather than one in which women for the moment dominate, the edit would have been clear and logical. We would have gone from the murder to the murderer, but in this instance we go from the murder to someone who pretends a man, not a woman, committed the murder and then, when that does not work, pretends to be the murderer herself to protect her daughter. The traditional editing logic that leads from the car driving off to the person doing the driving goes astray, and we are led off the path of clear knowledge, the kind that by rationally and logically pursuing consequences to causes, a murder victim to a murderer, maintains moral order. The work of woman in the film is to betray the editing logic and, with it, the moral logic. This explains why the end of the film is filled with such intense images of visual order, with the most important being the one in which Veda, the monster girl, is finally caught legally as well as visually, placed between a cured mother and a curing father/detective in a block of light that fixes boundaries around her that she never before possessed, while separating her from the emotional doubling with her mother that got her into trouble in the first place. But a doubling of sorts is still at work. Veda goes off to prison, and so as well, in a way, does Mildred.

Films about men frequently deal with the question of masculinity, that standard of male behavior that mandates toughness, independence, adventurousness, and freedom from "weak" emotions as appropriately masculine virtues. It also determines that sensitivity, passivity, domesticity, and emotional dependence are feminine traits that must be avoided if masculinity is to be achieved or safeguarded. That masculinity might be characterized as an "achievement" rather than as an assumed natural reality with a settled ontological status as part of being, however, already suggests some of the problems that haunt it as a cultural and psychological standard.

Many of the travails of masculinity have as much to do with psychology as sociology. And there are, as a result, several contending ways of accounting for them. The initial relationship with its mother provides the child with his sense of self, his ego identity. According to the psychoanalytic model, boys, in order to become men, must learn to separate from their mother; the male child must accept separation from the mother. This separation allows him to identify with his father and to assume his "proper" gender identity.

Because women traditionally performed the labor of raising children (and still do in most households), male children are presented with an initial maternal object of identification that is quite different from the one the culture they inhabit says they must achieve. This early maternal model for behavior modeling must, therefore, be discarded. Male gender identity is formed out of an initial experience of contact with a caring maternal body that negates or threatens its ultimate goal of emulating the ideal of masculinity lodged in a father. Boys quickly learn, at school if not at home, that to be "like your mother" is not acceptable or appropriate in a culture that requires that boys conform to standards of "manliness." Because fathers are traditionally assigned work outside the home that mandates toughness, independence, and competitiveness as indispensable tools for survival, the paternal masculine model is usually purged of traits such as empathy, sensitivity of response, and a capacity for care that connote weakness and vulnerability. Thus, despite

FIGURE 12.3 *Fight Club* (1999). A man is hugged by a very maternal man in an empathy group in this film about male gender identity.

an early conditioning in the hands of mothers, boys must learn to shed all traces of behavior they might have learned from female caregivers who are conditioned to be more empathetic, sensitive, and caring in regard to children. Men cannot be what they (initially) are if they are to become what they (ultimately) must be. Masculinity will therefore always be characterized by a fear or rejection of femininity or of the caring maternal body. It will also be characterized by uncertainty.

One senses quickly in a gendered culture of this sort that to "be" anything is to be a copy of a copy. We emulate ideals that are lodged in people who themselves are as they are because they emulated ideals lodged in others back through social history. As a result, depictions of men and of masculinity frequently concern efforts to achieve a reassuring natural ground for gender identity, one that would make the copy seem like an original or the fabricated cultural ideal seem real. These efforts both reveal and work to conceal the fact that male gender identity is haunted by the possibility of unreality, emptiness, failure, and impossibility. As a result, it is also fraught with panic, hysteria, anxiety, and fear.

There is thus a lethal element of uncertainly in the male child's gender experience. One consequence is that film stories about male identity often contain highly charged encounters with external threats to masculinity that are metaphors for this internal uncertainty. Such encounters often are characterized by violence that both purges the threats and provides a surrogate sense of grounding and solidity that cures the sense of emptiness and unreality that haunts masculine identity. Heightened experiences, usually physical in character, take the place of a successfully achieved gender grounding. As in *Fight Club*, the physical contact in violence provides a surrogate, a sense of natural, bodily substance, that fills the absence left by the necessary departure from the mother in male maturation.

Student Assignment 1: *Thelma and Louise*

How does the film draw on till-now male genres such as the buddy movie and the western in its depiction of the two women's flight? What visual motifs are used to draw attention to those genres? For example, landscape and open space were used in westerns to evoke the conflict between individual striving and a nature that lent credence to male gender ideals. How is that the case in this film? Pay special attention to the editing between different kinds of space in the film. With what kinds of space are men usually associated? How is that juxtaposed to the spaces in which Thelma and Louise find themselves?

Characterization and character transformation are essential to the film. How are the two women initially characterized? As the film progresses, each changes. How would you characterize those transformations? How does the film draw attention to the role-like nature of our identities? Roles often have to do with costumes and with rehearsed behavior. Where do you see rehearsal and costume in the film operating as important elements of character transformation?

Given those issues, one of the interesting lines Hal, the police detective, utters is "Behave yourself." It suggests submission to discipline, and he certainly represents

FIGURE 12.4 *Thelma and Louise.* Two women assume traditional male roles both socially and cinematically.

the discipline of the law as well as the idea that men in power in society have imposed a kind of discipline on women. The phrase can also imply "behave like yourself," as in "play the role you are assigned." Where in the film can you find indications that the women's departure from the law is in some respects a departure from assigned roles?

Finally, why does the film's narrative require the ending that is given? Could the film have ended differently?

Student Assignment 2: *Reservoir Dogs*

How is the film a meditation on male gender identity? How are unemotional toughness and empathetic care juxtaposed? How does the film emphasize the performative dimension of masculinity?

FIGURE 12.5 *Reservoir Dogs*. Gangsters taunt each other regarding masculinity.

FURTHER READING

Chevannes, Barry. *Learning To Be A Man*. Barbados: University of the West Indies Press, 2001.

Chodorow, Nancy. *Individualizing Gender and Sexuality*. New York: Routledge, 2012.

Hines, Sheila, and Tam Sanger. *Transgender Identities: Towards a Social Analysis of Gender Diversity*. New York: Routledge, 2010.

Lee, Julian. *Policing Sexualities*. New York: Zed Books, 2011.

Lockford, Lesa. *Performing Femininity*. Oxford: AltaMira Press, 2004.

Penner, James. *Pinks, Pansies, and Punks: The Rhetoric of Masculinity*. Bloomington: Indiana University Press, 2011.

Pfaff, Donald. *Man and Woman: An Inside Story*. New York: Oxford University Press, 2011.

Ethnic Criticism

Racism has its roots in human evolution. In early human history, humans needed minds that protected them from predators, and often those predators were other early human groups. Those minds were oriented toward defensiveness regarding potential adversaries. They monitored the world for signs of danger and learned to consider those very different from themselves as potential threats. Survival depended on the ability to secure resources in competition with other groups and to form alliances with in-group members to secure and protect resources against out-group people. One way of understanding contemporary racism is to see it as a residue of this adaptive ability to survive by bonding with one's group against other competing groups. The members of those other groups were seen as threats, not kin.

As humans developed agriculture and became capable of living in large settlements and communities, new cognitive abilities were required. We had to be able to see those very different from us as kin or as fellow citizens. We became capable of imagining other people and of empathizing with them. That allowed us to live cooperatively with them in civil communities. To do that, our minds had to be capable of designing universal principles of justice as well as universally binding rules that applied equally to all, not just to our buddies in our in-group. At the same time we became capable of creating cultural stories such as Greek tragedies that taught us the norms we needed to know in order to live in the new, more humane, more civil communities. We developed an ability to treat others as equals, even if they did not belong to our group. And we acquired the ability to restrain and to control our ancestral urges towards defensive hostility towards out-group people.

But not all humans evolved these new cognitive capacities to the same degree. All still possessed the more primitive disposition of fearful defensiveness in regard to strangers, but some had less of it than others, and some had more of the capacity to empathize. The conflict between the two dispositions has characterized human society for several millennia, and it may help account for the difference between liberals and conservatives. Liberals and conservatives have been found to differ physiologically, and such physiological differences are signs of different evolutionary trajectories. Liberals possess a larger anterior cingulate cortex than conservatives, who possess a larger amygdala. The amygdala is the seat of emotion and is located at the top of the spine, suggesting it was one of the first parts of the brain to evolve, and its functions may be linked to early human needs such as predator avoidance and to basic human drives such as self-preservation. That would explain another finding of recent brain science: the presence of a greater fear of death in conservatives. A greater death fear would allow one to flee predators more successfully. It would be more likely to be found in those with a larger amygdala (which regulates feelings of fight or flight), and it would explain why conservatives focus on the defense of one's resources against competitors. More than liberals, conservatives resist taxation whose purpose is to help others. One's own survival comes first. Conservatives also evidence more distrust of ethnic others, especially in regard to immigration. A more active amygdala has been found to be associated with greater levels of racial prejudice. In contrast, the anterior cingulate cortex is associated with the regulation of negative emotions and with less racial prejudice, and having more of that cortex may explain why liberals are less prone than conservatives to hostility towards ethnic others and immigrants. Their comparatively diminished fear of death suggests less of a need for defensive aggression against perceived adversaries.

Conservatism in the US has traditionally been the political philosophy of large property owners. But working class people whose economic lives are precarious and unstable tend as well to embrace conservative positions. It is easier to blame government taxation or competing ethnic groups for economic hardship than an invisible economic system that allocates rewards unequally. That has been especially true in the contemporary era in the US, a period characterized by an enormous decline in the economic fortunes of such men and women. The increasing presence of recent immigrant groups in the US that compete for scarce resources on the bottom rungs of the income ladder has contributed to the feelings of resentment and anger such men and women experience, feelings that make hostility to ethnic mixture and multicultural pluralism more attractive.

Falling Down dramatizes these issues from the point of view of a conservative white American male who has lost his job and his family and who feels resentment against new immigrant groups. Bill castigates an Asian-American grocer, for example, for not being sufficiently American, and he gets into a fight with Latino gang members when he challenges their cultural assumptions. The film seems to endorse the man's harshly Americanist feelings about ethnicity (by, for example, adding yellow light to the scene with the Asian grocer that recalls the nineteenth-century cultural stereotype of the "yellow peril," the idea that Asians pose a particular threat to white Americans). He is initially linked visually to two emblems of conservative white Christian culture, the ideal of individual freedom and the Christ story of personal suffering and sacrifice. As he waits in a frustrating traffic jam at the beginning of the film, he looks at bumper stickers that mention "freedom" and "he died for your sins." In this film, the white American male has lost his freedom, and he does die standing up for his rights against a multiethnic society whose corruption and inhumanity is lent a particularly conservative and right-wing populist codification, from Asian-American grocers who charge too much for a Coke to public workers who do make-work jobs to keep the public tax money flowing, and to wealthy people who enjoy leisure while hard-working lower-class men struggle.

In the film, white American males are portrayed as under attack from a harsh economic climate, hostile non-white ethnic groups, and women who emasculate them because they do not possess financial power. Bill complains that he is no longer "economically viable," but no cause is given for his loss of economic status. That lack of information or explanation befits, however, a consciousness that fails to pierce the empirical economic reality around it and is incapable of deciphering the structural causes of its own suffering. Instead, it turns its anger and resentment against more empirically visible surface annoyances, such as a truculent Asian-American grocer or excess government spending, that are misread as structural causes.

In contrast, Prendergast's sidekick is a sympathetically portrayed young Hispanic woman who admires him. While Bill gets enraged at ethnic minority grocers and street gang members, Prendergast in contrast more rationally accepts his ethnic minority partner. The strategy of placing two quite different characters in similar situations or relations allows the film to indulge in an exploration of racist attitudes while nevertheless appearing to endorse a much more anti-racist position embodied in the police detective.

The strategy is at work especially in the sequence in the used military supply store. The owner is a neo-Nazi racist and homophobe, and, before Bill kills him, he characterizes him as a "sick motherfucker" in contrast to himself: "I'm an American." This differentiation has the effect of distancing the more extreme forms of ethnic hatred associated with the radical Right, while nevertheless lending endorsement to Bill's more mainstream conservative "American" brand of ethnic animosity, which he turns against the "extremes" of the street gang and the rude, unhelpful, and apparently exploitative grocer.

The visual portrayal of the characters in the two scenes of ethnic conflict endows Bill with a sense of virtue and respectability, while the non-white characters are made to appear "greasy," dark, threatening, vicious, uncivil, and irrational. Tellingly, for an evolutionary understanding of racism, they are also made to appear animalistic. Bill wears a white shirt and tie, has a neat haircut, and is lit usually in such a way as to make his actions and statements appear rational and virtuous. Mr. Lee, the grocer, is in contrast dressed in a motley dark shirt that appears too tight, he is unshaven and rough looking, and lit in such a way as to connote deceptiveness and incivility. His dark store seems more the cave of a brute animal than a well-lit and transparent place of fair dealing. His windows, drawing on an old racist code for Asians, are yellow. In one image, he is juxtaposed to a porcelain pig. The young Hispanic men circle Bill like prowling animals on the hunt while he sits and minds his own business. Their faces in close-up are dark and sweaty, another emblem of animality, and their hair is thick with oil. When they ride in a car together, they resemble howling animals.

FIGURE 13.1 *Falling Down*. The Asian-American grocer is associated with a porcelain pig.

Such a cognitive lowering of one's adversaries from human to animal is one way to expel ethnic adversaries from the group of protected fellow humans in regard to whom one has evolved adaptive attitudes of cooperation rather than competition and aggression. To belong to an ethnic group is to identify oneself with others who are like oneself. But adversaries are pushed outside the group of accepted companions. They are often, as in this film, lowered in status from human to animal and made to appear wild and irrational. This would explain why the Asian-American grocer is associated with a pig and why the Hispanic gang members are portrayed as baring fangs like wild animals. The negative images of ethnic adversaries are projections of fear. A fear response in regard to ethnic others would be an expected evolutionary adaptation in an environment in which different groups competed for scarce resources. The fear response prepares the members of a group to be defensively antagonistic towards a group that might challenge their resources and threaten their survival. It is noteworthy, for example, that Bill asks Mr. Lee for change so that he can telephone his ex-wife, who is pictured with groceries (resources) in the background of her kitchen. And his conflict with Mr. Lee arises because he does not have enough money (resources) for the telephone call.

Mockery of others is another way to lower them in status and to expel them from the group of protected affines or kin. Mean humor is used to make acts of destruction and cruelty on Bill's part appear comic. Laughter is provoked by his use of a baseball bat to smash Mr. Lee's goods and "reduce" his prices after asking how much they cost. The Latino boys are made to look silly when Bill pulls out his club and chases them away. When the Latino boys crash their car and are lying on the ground, their weapons around them, Bill picks up a gun and gives one of them a lesson in shooting straight by shooting him in the leg. Such mean humor is, of course, itself an expression of violent feelings toward others. It gives expression to the harsh evolutionary law of survival—that to survive as a group, one must look down upon and be willing to "put down" (both verbally and physically) threats to one's group. Mean humor is a form of such putting down. Making someone an object of laughter demeans him.

Hostility towards out-groups was an adaptation that aided survival in the evolution of Homo sapiens. That would explain why racism is such a common feature of human societies and why it manifests itself at times of economic difficulty when survival is precarious. In a sense we are all racists (or would-be racists) simply by virtue of being human organisms whose ancestors survived and reproduced. They survived because they evolved defensive mechanisms to protect them from strangers. In conservative films like *Falling Down*, one is more likely to find evidence of continuing racism because of how conservatives and liberals seem to have differently evolved. With larger amygdalae and smaller anterior cingulate cortexes, conservatives are less likely to feel empathy for the suffering of members of competing ethnic groups. With larger cingulate cortexes and smaller amygdalae, liberals are more likely to feel such empathy. These differences in attitudes toward ethnic others are adaptive and have their roots in humans' ancestral past.

Student ASSIGNMENT: *Hate* (1995)

This liberal film is critical of racism. How is racism depicted as being harmful? What is the point of the joke about the man falling from a building? How does the film depict a relationship between racial animosity and economics?

FIGURE 13.2 *Hate*. In this film about an Arab, a Jew, and an African who are friends, the boys try to renounce violence, but it is forced upon them.

FURTHER READING

Alba, Richard. *Ethnic Identity: The Transformation of White America*. New Haven: Yale University Press, 1990.

Davids, M. Fakhree. *Internal Racism*. New York: Palgrave, 2011.

Schlee, Gunther. *Imagined Differences: Hatred and the Construction of Identity*. New York: Palgrave, 2002.

Smith, Robert C. *Conservatism and Racism*. Albany: State University of New York Press, 2010.

Verkuyten, M. *The Social Psychology of Ethnic Identity*. New York: Psychology Press, 2005.

Political Criticism

Politics derives from the Greek word *polis* or city, and it names the way governance is conducted and power exercised in communities. The most obvious kind of politics is the institutional life of governments. But there is also a more general politics of everyday life concerning struggles over values, customs, norms, roles, standards of behavior, and the distribution of wealth and social power. This broader kind of politics is carried out in public debates, in social movements, in discussions at workplaces, in magazines and journals, and in the media. In this broad sense, everything that might involve a choice of value or a change in the way society is organized and run is "political." Politics usually consists of the attempt to influence others to adopt particular ideas or to support certain values. In this sense, politics is indistinguishable from rhetoric, the use of language to change people's beliefs.

Politics often divides between left and right. The left or liberal side favors ideals of community, cooperation, and equality, a broad conception of human and civil rights that should be protected from political authority, a strong sense of economic fairness, and a concept of government as the embodiment of the community's democratically determined wishes. The right or conservative side locates a core value in individual freedom in economic matters. Conservatives believe economic markets do a better job of allocating resources and solving social problems than governments. Conservatives favor a meritocratic image of society that justifies economic inequality ("winners" versus "losers"). And they believe in traditional religious values and traditional social forms, such as the patriarchal family. They are usually hostile to an expansion of rights and are more likely to accept authoritarian political forms.

Conservatives in the late twentieth century believed that the socialist and communist ideal of economic equality was a threat to personal "freedom" and to capitalism. One of the most salient political differences and conflicts of the twentieth century had to do with economic inequality. Conservatives felt it was a necessary and reasonable outcome of a capitalist economic system; liberals and socialists felt economic inequality should be remedied or eliminated entirely through government action that emphasized cooperation over competition. The conservative position was also an individualist one. Inequality was justified because it arose from differences in individual talent. Left alone by governments to exercise their abilities, individuals rise or fall to the position in life they deserve. The emotional tone of this position was tough-minded. There was little room for emotions such as empathy. Losers deserved what they got, as did winners. When the competitive economic game is fair, no one should expect sympathy or assistance from the government.

Liberals and socialists countered by claiming that all economies and all societies are interconnected wholes. For some to rise in a capitalist economy, many must be kept down and condemned to lives of labor without much reward. Changing that situation and bringing about more egalitarian societies became a goal of twentieth century leftism. The conservative right wing responded with movements such as Fascism and Nazism that used violence and authoritarianism to maintain inequality. But the political left often mounted violent revolutions of its own that were socialist or communist in character. They advocated the use of government to remedy economic inequality. Often those movements overlapped with movements against colonial rule and were called national liberation movements. Such was the case in Vietnam from the late 1940s to the mid-1970s.

The Vietnam War occasioned severe divisions in the US between those who favored ending the war because it was unjust and those who wished to pursue a more violent strategy designed to win. American involvement in the Vietnam War began when the national liberation forces in Vietnam defeated the French, their colonial rulers, in 1954. A peace conference divided the country between a north controlled by the liberation forces and a south controlled by a government controlled by the US. The US-backed regime never honored the call issued by the peace conference for elections to unite the country because it was clear that the northern candidate, Ho Chi Minh, a charismatic national liberation fighter, would win. When the north invaded the south, the US was drawn in militarily to defend its puppet regime. When that regime began to fail, the US overthrew it and replaced it with military rulers. Increasingly, the US was drawn into the conflict and had to fight the war with its own forces. Liberals argued that this was a mistake, while conservatives argued for more forceful measures to assure victory.

Apocalypse Now is a highly rhetorical film that argues for a forceful resolution to the war. Written and directed by two of America's leading right wing filmmakers, Francis Ford Coppola and John Milius, and appearing four years after the war ended in 1975, the film frames the military argument in terms that echo the economic individualism of conservative political philosophy that was coming to dominate American public discourse in the late 1970s. Coppola and Milius frame their individualist and militarist argument in religious and racialist terms. Asia is portrayed as a haven of primitive barbarism, its Buddhist religion linked to blood sacrifice and mindless violence, while the "mission" of the heroic American soldier, Willard, is framed as a quest narrative with resonances in the medieval Fisher King story and the Christ story. The white and the fair-haired are good and civilized, while the dark and the short are faceless, voiceless incarnations of brutal, primeval, savage urges. Most remarkable about the film is the degree to which it integrates the conservative critique of liberalism to the war story. Heroism consists of withstanding liberal bureaucracy and governmental inefficiency in favor of an individualist warrior-leader ideal. The warrior hero is a conservative free market entrepreneur in disguise.

The film's narrative maps a trajectory from weakness to strength. At the outset, Willard, an army hit-man, is weak and drunk in a hotel room in Saigon, a city associated with "shit." By the end of the film, he will embrace a warrior ideal of "clean" brutality for the sake of victory. That ideal is superimposed as overlay images of his face from later in the film when, having dunked himself in the water of the primeval swamp and emerged the color of the natives, he is reborn and ready for the warrior task of killing Colonel Kurtz and fulfilling his mission. That mission has a religious meaning of renewing the community through blood sacrifice. By the end, he has passed over to the side of dark skin and moral evil, the ability to kill cleanly and without conscience that Kurtz imputes to the national liberation forces.

When Willard is given his assignment to find and kill Kurtz, Kurtz is linked to Christ. It begins to become clear almost immediately that Kurtz's individualism, visionary leadership, and warrior abilities are unacceptable to an Army bureaucracy that dines well, while the enemy gets by on rat meat and will accept nothing short of victory or death. America needs to adopt a similar attitude in order to be "saved," according to the filmmakers, mistaking a difference between colonial invaders with no motive for winning and liberation forces with a strong motive for fighting hard to free their homeland as a difference between races. Much of the narrative between the assignment and the killing consists of episodes meant to portray the war as being lost by liberal, bureaucratic ineptitude. What is needed, the filmmakers argue, is strong visionary leadership by a conservative individualist that transcends bureaucratic procedures, legal rules, civilian democratic protest, and the restraints of moral conscience.

FIGURE 14.1 *Apocalypse Now*. The individualist must cut through governmental bureaucracy with force, an indication of how the film is as much about domestic American economic politics as it is about foreign policy.

The first episode on the journey concerns a military unit that captures coastal villages so as to be able to surf, a sign that the war is not being conducted with appropriate seriousness or ruthlessness. The next episode portrays the regular army as populated by unprofessional non-warriors (a cook in this instance) who should have stayed at home. The next concerns an entertainment by Playboy Bunnies, semi-naked women who distract the army from its mission by dancing erotically in front of the troops, a scene which ends in a riot. In this episode as well, bureaucracy is portrayed as corrupting the war effort, and Willard is obliged to use physical force to cut through the "red tape" to get supplies that he needs. In another episode expunged from the original version, the boat encounters a leaderless camp where the Playboy Bunnies cavort with the soldiers in exchange for fuel oil. The war effort, in other words, is sacrificed for personal pleasure. Conservatives in the 1970s depicted liberals (especially those of the generation of the 1960s) as overly "permissive" in regard to sexuality and personal morality. The next episode depicts a French plantation whose right wing owners are depicted favorably and who complain that the US is allowing student protest to prevent it from winning, another negative reference to the generation of the 1960s which was characterized by student protests against the Vietnam War. In another episode, Willard is obliged to kill a wounded Vietnamese woman to prevent the captain of his boat from turning around to take her to a hospital. No misguided liberal empathy should interfere with the mission, the sequence argues. At the final bridge before entering Kurtz's territory, there is also no leader, and half the men are on drugs, another sign of the regular Army's failure.

As he travels on, Willard comes increasingly to identify with Kurtz, the man he is supposed to assassinate. He comes to see him as a heroic, warrior individualist who is a seer-leader capable of winning the war on his own by adopting the enemy's guerrilla tactics. In conservative eyes, such leaders should be obeyed because they possess superior intuitive abilities and innate authority. Liberal bureaucracy is wrong because it curtails the individual leader's will. And indeed the background battle in the film, contained in Kurtz's dossier, which Willard reads as he makes his journey, is between the liberal rule-makers and the radical individualist who "goes for himself" and seeks to win the war on his own. That his methods prove to be successful suggests to what extent the film endorses the conservative ideal of a authoritarian leader.

At Kurtz's camp, Kurtz recounts a tale in which US Special Forces are portrayed as humanitarian saviors while the Vietnamese are portrayed as doing violence to their own people. The US soldiers vaccinate children, but the Vietnamese soldiers return and cut off the vaccinated arms. "If I had ten divisions of those men," he says, "all our problems here would be over in no time." The argumentative strategy is to assign to national liberation fighters an ideal of military brutality that wins wars, while suggesting that the liberals who oppose that conservative military ideal are the ones responsible for the war being "lost." Willard provides an example of how to perform this changeover from weakness to ruthless strength by completing his mission and

FIGURE 14.2 *Apocalypse Now*. An American solider must learn what true soldiering is all about by "going native," adopting the local skin color, and becoming more "barbaric" like the Vietnamese in this very racist film.

murdering Kurtz. To do so, he must dunk himself in the swamp and emerge colored like a native. The murder itself is paralleled to the sacrifice of a bull. Kurtz also reads Jessie Weston's *From Ritual to Romance*, and *The Waste Land*, a famous poem by T. S. Eliot, both of which refer to the legend of the Fisher King. The King is the mythical keeper of the Holy Grail who must either be healed or replaced by the questing Grail Knight. Willard is thus associated with rebirth and with the sacrifice of the old king so that a new one can take his place. Fittingly, the natives bow down to him as their new ruler once he kills Kurtz.

The film's argument is situated within a context of discussion regarding the Vietnam War that pitted conservatives against liberals. In some respects, it is a retrospective film that looks back on the war, but is also a prospective one, in that the argument in 1979 and beyond (all the way down to the re-release of the expanded version in 2001) would continue to characterize foreign policy debates. It should be paired with the documentary *Hearts and Minds* (1975) that tells the story of the war from the point of view of the Vietnamese. A very different picture of the war emerges once you cross the line dividing "us" from "the enemy" and begin listening to their account of the war. Instead of an allegorical conflict between weak Western liberal principles of legal warfare and strong, ruthless, and efficient Eastern principles of warfare that we would do well to emulate, what one encounters in this film is a complex sense of the historical reality of the war. The link back to French colonialism is presented not as the continuation of a heroic struggle against restless natives but as the brutal, exploitative suppression of an indigenous population for the sake of access to raw materials for the Western economy. Moreover, the equation between Eastern Buddhist religion and military ruthlessness is contradicted by the voices of Buddhist monks in the documentary who speak reasonably about their opposition to colonialism and to the imposition of a military government on the South Vietnamese by the US. While the opponents of the US are presented in *Apocalypse Now* as the practitioners of ruthless violence, in the documentary what emerges is a sense that the US and its South Vietnamese allies were in fact the greater wrongdoers in this regard.

Student Assignment: *The Official Story* (1985)

The troubled economies of Latin America spawned many egalitarian movements that occasionally attained or nearly gained political power in the period after World War II. The response by American conservatives like Henry Kissinger (Secretary of State at the time) was to support military coups that kept economic elites in power. Liberals were critical of these actions and of the enormous loss of life and of civil liberties that they entailed. But knowledge of the events was frequently curtailed by policies of official secrecy. Many of the most violent acts, such as the forced "disappearance" (kidnapping, torture, and murder) of egalitarians, labor unionists, progressive nuns and priests, and human rights activists in places like Argentina after its coup in 1976, were kept from public knowledge. Only after the military junta was overturned in Argentina and a Truth Commission agreed to trade amnesty for information did the facts emerge. In Argentina alone, during the "dirty war" against economic egalitarians from 1976 to 1983, anywhere from 10,000 to 30,000 people "disappeared." (See the documentary *Las Madres de la Plaza de Mayo* and the Wikipedia entry for the "Dirty War," as well as the New York

I awoke naked on a table.
They began torturing me.

FIGURE 14.3 *The Official Story.* A woman learns that a friend was tortured by a US-backed military dictatorship.

Times, October 8, 2011, Alexei Barrionuevo, "Daughter of Dirty War Raised by Man Who Killed Parents.")

The Official Story deals with these issues. It concerns a woman who discovers that her adopted child was taken from one of the "disappeared" and that her husband is complicit in crimes against humanity. How is Alicia's story of personal enlightenment also a story about political enlightenment? How does she change in the course of the movie?

FURTHER READING

McSherry, J. Patrice. *Predatory States: Operation Condor and Covert War in Latin America*. Lanham: Rowland and Littlefield Publishers, 2005.

Menjivar, Cecilia, and Nestor Rodriguez. *When States Kill: Latin America, the U.S., and Technologies of Terror*. Austin: University of Texas Press, 2005.

Ware, Alan. *Political Conflict in America*. New York: Palgrave MacMillan, 2011.

15 CHAPTER

Poststructuralist Criticism

Poststructuralism extrapolated from the ideas of Structuralism, especially the idea that differences create identities. The Structuralists said language consists of word-sounds whose identity is given by their difference from other word-sounds. "Hat" has no identity of its own as a word-sound in the English language apart from its difference from similar words like "mat" and "cat." Only a slight difference makes "hat" meaningful and provides it with an identity as a word. Poststructuralist philosophers like Jacques Derrida applied this notion to how we think about the world. All of our ideas come into being and acquire an identity through differences from other ideas. Derrida used examples from philosophy such as "truth," "being," and "beauty." When philosophers in the past tried to define them, they had to rely on comparisons that differentiated those ideas from other ideas. But those other ideas were themselves tangled up in differences. Nowhere could a clear identity of anything be found in the realm of ideas that did not give rise to more differences. Our ideas seem clear and true, but they rest on a sea of differences that we must ignore if we are to use our ideas in everyday life.

The difference principle applies to everyday ideas such as "freedom." "Freedom" should line up with a thing in the word that it names. That would be its identity, and the thing it names should have a similar identity, one with a clear boundary designating an inside from an outside, all that belongs to "freedom" from all that does not. But the supposed identity of freedom quickly becomes differential. It has a number of meanings that differ depending on the situation in which they occur. One meaning of the idea is that it names our ability to choose political leaders. That certainly makes Americans more free than, say, the people of China. But another particularly American meaning of freedom is economic. And in the work world, some are more free than others. The wealthy can spend entire days doing nothing if they choose. The poor cannot. Freedom is a relative quantity, in other words, not an absolute one with a clear identity. It is constituted by differences of degree and comparative relations with other terms and a diversity of situations. About its identity, one can only say "it depends." It is one thing in one context, another in a different context. To know the identity of freedom, you would have to take such differences and such relative gradients (more/less) into account. Freedom would start to have fuzzy, unclear edges, rather than a clear and distinct identity that distinguishes it from other ideas and things. In the work world, freedom even begins to blend with

207

its opposite—authoritarianism. The freedom of the capitalist to fire workers to make his operation more efficient hinges on their complete lack of freedom and on his complete authority over them.

Poststructuralism is often associated with liberal pragmatism, the philosophy that sees ideas working differently in different contexts or situations. There are no absolute, purely abstract or ideal meanings for ideas. They have no meaning outside of the situations in which they occur; they are flexible tools that perform different tasks in different contexts. "Freedom" is a useful tool in opposing political authoritarianism, but it is less useful in talking about economics, where one person's freedom means another person's lack of freedom. Many prefer to think there is clarity in the world of ideas. The ocean of differential relations, nuances of context, and gradients of meaning is supervised by lighthouses that bring clarity to the world of thought—and with it a sense of authority. Clear ideas match up with clear things, and that puts an end to difference and to debate. Freedom is an accurate name for a real identity in the world. Such beliefs provide a sense of authority and put uncertainty to rest.

But for authority to work in this way, quelling debate and annulling difference, it must itself be outside the field of debate regarding the meaning of ideas like freedom. Otherwise, it is just one more opinion. "God" operated as such a point of transcendent authority in traditional societies, and in daily life in traditional patriarchal societies, "father" served as the point of authority, the person who declared things to be the case and put an end to discussion.

Poststructuralism consists of a critical examination of such ideals of transcendence. It deconstructs the pretense to authority in our ideas about the world (and by implication in our institutional lives that are justified by ideas). Usually, it points out that such authority rests on an ideal of identity that supposedly transcends difference. But the differential relations that give any idea its identity cannot be transcended. To acknowledge that, however, would be to turn oneself into a liberal pragmatist, someone who sees ideas as differing in meaning depending on the webs of differential relations, the context, in which they operate. That is why it is so important for those with an investment in authority to deny the difference principle. A lot depends on it, not least the authorities that pretend to supervise our lives.

How does all of this apply to movies? Movies argue in favor of values, and values are choices amongst contending alternative possibilities for framing and understanding the world. Those choices often present themselves as absolute points of authority. They seem to have an identity that is untouched by dependence on something else, another possible framing of the world, or another understanding of it. But, in fact, many values promoted in film are debatable rather than absolute because they differ with and differ from alternate possible ways of constructing understandings of the world. Are Arabs who oppose US interests terrorists or freedom fighters? Were Americans heroic liberators in Iraq or arrogant neo-imperialists? It depends. None of the possibilities is absolutely true. All are connected to frames of understanding, other alternative ways of formulating what counts as real and true, and that contingency is rendered invisible by the force with which the claim of absolute authority is asserted.

The Godfather, for example, strives to convince its audience that male patriarchal authority is needed in order to save the world. This ideal of authority is portrayed as something singular unto itself, an identity that is not the product of a conflict of frames or interpretations—of differences and relations. Rather, it is above such rhetorical combat; it is not one opinion among others. It stands outside and above all such differences of opinion, all such contending alternative frames of understanding. It is an ultimate transcendent authority.

Fittingly, *The Godfather* begins with a scene in which the Don of a mafia family remains in a room apart from others at a wedding feast. He is aloof, separate, a transcendental authority that does not mix with others. His identity is unsullied by relations. This separation is a metaphor for the film's point that no other possible way of constructing the world exists. Patriarchy is absolutely true and absolutely necessary. But the film both labors to establish this ideal of authority and inadvertently reveals that it is in fact contingent. It is produced in the film through a series of differentiations that imply that it is one alternative possibility among many for framing and understanding the world.

The film tells the story of a mafia family that undergoes a crisis and survives by ridding itself of its enemies within the gangster community. The crisis is set going when Don Corleone is approached by another mobster named Salazzo about entering the narcotics business. The Don refuses because he wishes to preserve the family's more traditional business endeavors, and Salazzo tries to have him killed. A war results during which Salazzo is murdered by Don Corleone's youngest son, Michael. Michael goes into exile in Sicily, while Sonny, his older brother, runs the family business. But Sonny is himself murdered, and Michael, who has married a Sicilian woman who is assassinated in an attempt on his life, returns home to take charge of the family. His ailing father, Don Corleone, counsels him that he will eventually be the object of an assassination attempt. Michael foils the attempt and succeeds in eliminating his foes. In a side plot, he marries his old non-Italian girlfriend, Kay, and, in the end, when she asks if he indeed had his brother-in-law killed for having helped the family enemies, he says no. But the audience has just witnessed his execution of the brother-in-law. The triumphal achievement of power by Michael is paralleled to an ejection of women from the world of male "business."

The film's moral universe is centered on the father. When sons question the father's authority, trouble ensues. The father successfully functions as an authority in this world if his will is unopposed and his pronouncements unquestioned. He provokes obedience, not dissent or difference. Indeed, difference is bad in this universe because it fragments the identity of authority the Godfather embodies.

But difference is everywhere at work making the Godfather possible. The Godfather is assigned identity by differentiations between loyalty and betrayal, men and women, the family and its others, pure business and the impurities of the personal, true godfathers and false godfathers. All of these differentiations are arranged hierarchically as oppositions, with the first value in each pair being superior to the second. All rest on a fundamental set of distinctions between the true and the false, the authentic and the artificial, the primary and the secondary,

FIGURE 15.1 *The Godfather.* Gestures of recognition give the Godfather his identity.

the original and the derived, the natural and the technical, presence and representation, substance and contrivance, an inside and an outside. Authority is guaranteed by the first term in each pair and betrayed by the second. What this means is that the authority the film strives to establish, which appears to be something solid and substantial in its own right, an identity that transcends all other possible ways of formulating social authority, instead arises from relations that are differential in character. It cannot be what it claims to be.

The identity of the Godfather rests on a relation to others in several ways. Most importantly, the godfather's authority requires that it be acknowledged by others. Without such acknowledgement, no authority would exist, and the Godfather would lose his identity as a point of authority. This might explain the importance of scenes of acknowledgement at both the beginning and the end of the film. In the first, an undertaker is reminded by Don Corleone that he has failed to acknowledge his authority. In the end, Michael, the new Don, is acknowledged by his subordinates who profess their loyalty to him. His identity is thereby confirmed, and the film comes full circle.

Such moments of acknowledgment or recognition are necessary and important because of the danger relations of dependence on other people pose. Loyalty is needed because the godfather depends on others and he is vulnerable to betrayal. Pauli, the Don's driver, betrays Don Corleone to Salazzo and allows him to be shot. Carlo, another outsider in relation to the family, betrays Sonny. The Godfather depends on others for the authority that only apparently resides within himself.

In order for the Godfather to function as an authority, this relation of dependence on others must be suppressed. When Michael cures the family crisis and assumes the role of Godfather, he arranges to have Carlo killed, just as Sonny had Pauli killed. More importantly, his assumption of power coincides with acts of violence against the others whose difference of opinion has endangered the authority of the Corleone family. In carrying out those acts of violence, he relies on loyal delegates who execute the rival family Dons in the concluding sequence of the film.

True Godfathers are distinguished from false Godfathers according to how well they can police the boundary between business and the personal, another crucial determiner of the Godfather's identity and of his supposedly transcendental authority. The good Godfather knows the family business and does not allow it to be contaminated with personal concerns. This difference is frequently configured as an opposition between mind and body. The good Godfather possesses powers of mind that allow him to intuitively guess when his adversaries will strike against him, while the bad Godfathers Sonny and Fredo are depicted as intemperate and promiscuous victims of bodily urges. Michael, on the other hand, performs all the traditional rituals and conventions of deference, respect, and courtship in his relationship with Apollonia in Sicily, and this is contrasted with the lecherous behavior of his bodyguards toward her. Moreover, in the end, Michael successfully deceives Kay, his wife, by telling her he did not have Carlo killed, after telling her it would be the one time he would allow her to intervene in family business. He thereby successfully uses his greater mental powers to distance the personal, bodily hysterics of his sister, Carlo's wife, which were the occasion for Sonny's downfall, and subordinates his personal loyalty to Kay to his loyalty to the family business.

The mind of the Godfather is thus portrayed as rising above and distinguishing itself from bodily passion, and authoritative leaders who have minds capable of grasping and exercising such powers can suppress emotion and personal attachments. Since social authority in this world is male, this means rising above women. Throughout, women are associated with theatricality, hysteria, non-seriousness, and the onset of crisis. At the moment of greatest crisis, when Don Corleone is shot, Michael, instead of being at home, is with Kay at the theater. Afterwards, she asks, "Would you like me better if I looked like Ingrid Bergman?" underscoring the association of women with a malleability, an artifice, and an instability of identity. After reading of the assassination attempt, he calls Sonny, whose first remark is that "There are lots of stories," as if a multiplication of different versions or representations coincided with the decapitation of the Don, with the loss of an identity of authority. When we first meet Michael, he is with Kay and dressed in another role, that of Army soldier, which differentiates him from his family. "That's my family, Kay, not me," he says, drawing attention to the way she leads him astray from his proper identity as family Godfather. When he finally acts to restore his family, he must separate from her and return to his ethnic and familial roots in Sicily, an ideal of nature that reinforces the idea of a natural family.

The policing of language by the true Godfathers and the constant reminders not to speak of family business to outsiders suggest how identity-based values are configured as relations between truth and other forms of language or representation. Language should be subordinate and secondary to truth in order for points of authority to be possible. But language can betray by representing things that are not the case or by leading people into arguments that undermine their singular authority. The first Don is undone when his words to Salazzo are not taken seriously, his offer of an agreement not accepted. The contracts of language can easily be broken. Sonny is weakest when he is arguing with a lawyer, someone associated with the use of language to contest truth. Truth is unstable and has no identity in his hands, and Sonny appears weak when he must argue his case.

Ideally, if the identity of authority resident in the Godfather is intact, such debate is unnecessary. The Godfather knows truth in himself, and when he speaks, others know as well what the truth is. This ideal of authority in language is overturned when Sonny is Don. Tom Hagen, the lawyer, argues with him and curtails his authority. When Michael assumes power, therefore, one of his first acts is to expel Tom. The event is not accidental; it bears essentially on the argument of the film inasmuch as it is about establishing the authority of the Godfather through the subordination of language to the Godfather's truth. The perfect relation between truth and language would be a command, a unity of word and act that delivers truth directly and without deviation. Embedded in the godfatherly ideal of society is a certain authoritarianism.

The Godfather is such a family man because in the family his speech can be fully and unequivocally authoritative. Danger arises when the Godfather's reach is extended beyond the boundary of the natural family. That danger is signaled in the joke in the film about an offer that cannot be refused—i.e., either your signature or your brains will be on this contract, said with a gun held to the person's head. The joke draws attention to the necessity of conforming one's will to external legal conventions to get one's way once the reach of the natural family is exceeded. One can no longer count on blood loyalty; one has to contract for loyalty instead. At that limit, the dependent relation on other people that is embodied in the idea of legal contract as the necessity of a mutual agreement, a reciprocal and equal exchange of vows, supersedes the direct embodiment of the male leader's will in the form of commands. The joke draws attention to the film's project of suppressing liberal legality in the name of the authoritative will of the leader. The violence of the gun to the head is merely an extension of the violence of the Godfather's words of command. The extralegality of the Godfather is a metaphor for the authority of individual will in conservative authoritarian political discourse.

This authoritarian vision of the world would have us believe that there is only one way of doing things, and that security lies in trusting our fates to strong political leaders. Poststructuralism suggests that this is just one particular opinion among many, rather than being a point of authority that must be believed and followed because it is absolute. The deconstructive method of analysis—which finds relations where there should only be identities—undermines the claim to authority by showing how the individual leader is less individual than he thinks. His life and his authority are constructed through dependent relations on others.

The point of Poststructuralism is that there exists a range of possible "authorities" for our norms, and we have to choose which to rely on. The argument of *The Godfather* is that that there is really only one such authority, and the patriarchal point of authority must be obeyed because the authority of the father is unquestionable, unique, and singular. There is none other like it. No alternative is possible. But this picture of the world posits identities that do not exist. They are not absolute but contingent; they depend on other things to be what they are—on loyal delegates, for example, or expressions of recognition and loyalty. The Godfather pretends to be a point of authority who stands apart from and above everyone else, but in truth, he would not be what he is, would not have the identity he claims for himself, if he were not connected in a dependent way on others. He is a convention, an agreement between terms, rather than an absolute and self-identical reality. His reality, his truth, is produced by the very things—differences from other people, for example—that seem secondary and derivative in relation to his identity.

Student ASSIGNMENT: *Run, Lola, Run* (1998)

Few films emphasize alternatives as well as *Run, Lola, Run*. The film is a meditation on the deeply connected character of people's lives, the fact that one life is contingent on another. Lola's actions affect the lives of those around her in seemingly random ways. The film explores the different possibilities set going by chance encounters with others. How, for example, do the lives of the bicyclist and the woman with the stroller change or evolve differently depending on when or how Lola encounters them?

Consider Lola's father. What does he represent and why is he in the film? How do her different arrival times in the three segments lead to very different outcomes in his conversation with his lover? Why is this the case? What point do you think the filmmakers are trying to make? We are left with a fairly large irony in regard to the

FIGURE 15.2 *Run, Lola, Run.* In this postmodern film, lovers debate the contingency of love and of existence.

father in the last segment. Why is it important to set up this joke at the expense of the father?

Poststructuralism promotes an ethic of care and responsibility. If everyone is seen as equally part of an inter-connected reality, then no one can claim to be superior and unique, a "Godfather." What are the ethics of this film?

FURTHER READING

Derrida, Jacques. "Différance," in *Speech and Phenomena*. Evanston: Northwestern University Press, 1973.

Postmodernism. New York: Films Media Group, 2005.

"Poststructuralism" and "Postmodernism" in *The Encyclopedia of Literary and Cultural Theory*. New York: Wiley-Blackwell, 2011.

Sim, Stuart. *The Routledge Companion to Postmodernism*. New York: Routledge, 2011.

Williams, James. *Understanding Poststructuralism*. Chesham: Acumen Publishers, 2005.

Woods, Tim. *Beginning Postmodernism*. Manchester: Manchester University Press, 2009.

Scientific Criticism: Evolutionary Theory

The human species is millions of years old. Our culture, however, our ability to do things like make meaningful marks on a page, is only about 40,000 years old. The kind of non-violent civilization regulated by laws that you take for granted is only about three thousand years old. That kind of civilization was made possible by changes in human cognition that allowed humans to adapt to their environment and to survive. As our ancestors began to live in larger agricultural communities, they needed institutions such as written laws, property rights, and shared norms of behavior to assure peace and harmony. The older urges in humans that moved them toward defensive violence against their fellows to safeguard scarce resources had to give way to more civil modes of interaction. People who in the past might have been considered threats to one's safety were now fellow citizens of a community. We were helped by our mind's ability to think in terms of abstract ideas and to see marks on a page as meaningful embodiments of ideas. We could now formulate laws—rules with ideas in them such as justice and fairness. We could safeguard our resources with words not weapons. The ability to think symbolically was crucial to this development in human evolution. The idea of property rights meant that one could leave one's farm field unguarded and no one would seize it. A new human institution called marriage assured that mating became a source of stability for the society. Fighting over mates gave way to a more peaceful process of cohabitation. The new family institution also assured that property would be passed on safely from one generation to the next and remain within the same family. With natural promiscuity put aside once and for all, one could know who was the father of a child. The cement of civilization—care for others—was created.

These new institutional arrangements were sustained by norms, by rules of behavior that all members of the community internalized as they grew up. Norms integrate us into a larger human community and make our behavior conform to its standards, standards that assure that the community will survive and not break down into violence that is detrimental to the survival of each member. Norms were first promulgated through religion, but eventually a culture of story-telling evolved that performed the same function. Greek tragedies were among the first uses of normative storytelling. The methods and techniques for telling stories have changed and continue to change. But many of the same kinds of stories are told now as were told in the past. We still love melodramas about personal dilemmas, evil villains who have no remorse, and threats to families. *2012* is about the apocalypse and required enormous computer generated imaging, but, shed the CGI and *2012* is a story about a threatened family that might have been found on any mid-nineteenth-century American stage. It concerns the norms that guide our behavior (with unselfish, pro-community behavior being praised, and selfishness that is detrimental to group survival being denigrated).

Many films are concerned with the norms that make humans human and human civilization civilized. Such films usually distinguish between good norm-sustaining behavior that supports civil institutions like the family and anti-normative behavior that threatens those institutions. A crime story is also a story about a breach in civilized norms, and a love story is about a natural mandate to reproduce that is orchestrated by civilized norms of ritualized courting behavior.

John Ford's *The Searchers* distinguishes between behavior that sustains human communities and behavior that is dangerous to them. It depicts the importance of norms in protecting such institutions as property and family. Such norms and institutions impose structure on nature, and the film, as you might expect, is highly structured both spatially and temporally. It begins with a frame within a frame, a doorway of a frontier cabin being opened onto a wide deep landscape by the mother of the family. The striking contrast between the dark enclosed interior and the open well-lit exterior suggests the fundamental conflict between a domestic, civilized world on the one hand and nature, with all the dangers it poses for civilization, on the other, that will be at the heart of the film. What the woman sees out in the landscape is her husband's brother, Ethan, returning from the Civil War. As he approaches the house, Ethan is depicted within a wide space dominated at either end by totemic outcroppings of rock, metaphors for the natural powers Ethan is associated with. He is a warrior who emerges out of nature. The framing emphasizes the vastness of the wilderness and implies that special qualities would be required to survive in it, but it also situates that world as "out there." The audience is positioned in the domestic world of civilization and community, which is framed as crowded with people at an orderly distance from each other and as protected by internal house frames. Civilized space is full space, and nature is empty and threatening.

In *The Searchers*, the core concern of human culture with making order out of natural disorder and civilization out of wild human behavior is an explicit theme. The film is laid out temporally as a series of quests into the wilderness to find a kidnapped white girl, and spatially as the symmetrical opposition between settler civilization and Native American Indian culture. If civilization is characterized by rules, norms, and community-building institutions such as monogamous marriage and property right, the natural wilderness is characterized by an apparent absence of such structures. It is a place where violence, not mutual care, guarantees survival and where the theft of property or bartering of women is the rule.

FIGURE 16.1 *The Searchers.* The movie opens with a visual contrast between nature and civilization.

After Ethan returns to the farm of his brother, Aaron, the farm is attacked by Natives. The family is murdered, and the two girls are kidnapped. One daughter eventually is murdered too, and Debbie, the youngest, becomes one of the wives of Chief Scar. Ethan and Marty, a half-breed adopted by Aaron, set out to find Debbie. Eventually they succeed, and Chief Scar is killed.

The two searchers make three quests. The first quest to find Debbie dramatizes the failure of the community to protect itself, and it separates Ethan from the others by demonstrating his superior knowledge of Native customs. Reverend Clayton, the embodiment of communal values and institutions, leads a large group of men after the Natives; they are attacked at a river; and when one is hurt, they realize that they must follow communal rules and save him by returning home. The very rules that make up the community disable it as an effective fighting force in the wilderness. In this part of the film, the men find a Native in a grave, an association that links the Natives to the natural world of physical matter, that which lies outside civil norms and institutions and which must be tamed by them.

The second quest is led by Ethan and takes the searchers into more dangerous territory than before, territory in which the assurances of civilized structure no longer are available and in which the dangers of nature become more pronounced. Those dangers also now become more explicitly codified in sexual terms. Ethan finds the body of Lucy, who, like her mother, has been sexually violated. That her body is found out of view and that he prevents Marty and Brad from going near it indicate that promiscuous sexuality can appear within civilization only in so far as it is repressed. As an emblem of "wild" nature, it is precisely what civilization cannot tolerate. Ethan's digging of the earth with his knife after he finds the body is suggestive of the connection between the physical body of sexuality and the physicality of nature. Appropriately, he covers her body with his army coat, a civilized symbol of the kind the community uses to repress and regulate the dangers of natural physical life. During this sequence as well, he engages in the civilized verbal repression of sexuality. When of Lucy Brad asks, "Was she … ?," meaning was she sexually violated, Ethan angrily responds: "Don't ask me again." And when he speaks of Debbie, he says that the Natives will "keep her to raise as one of their own, till she's of an age to …" He never pronounces the word. By repressing words associated with sexuality, he draws attention to the way physical sexual nature can only exist within the civilized community as something safely repressed or as something transmuted through the symbols and institutions of marriage.

Such marriage in the world of the movie presupposes an allocation of roles between "domestic" women and "masculine" men. And one danger that formless and undemarcated physical life poses to the structure of community-based civilization is that such roles might be undermined, the boundaries between them erased. Brad's lack of control when Ethan informs him of Lucy's murder is in contrast to Ethan's self-control. It deprives Brad of the criterion that will ultimately serve to qualify one as sufficiently masculine in the film—the ability to control wild natural emotions. But perhaps more importantly, it is associated with Ethan's remark that the person Brad sees wearing Lucy's dress is not in fact Lucy but a Native male dressing up as a woman. Amorphous physical nature not only undermines civilized patriarchal succession in the form of sexual promiscuity but also it works to confuse gender identities in such a way that masculinity becomes less easy to define and determine.

The successful rescue of Debbie coincides with a successful masculinization of Marty and with the symbolic building of a family predicated on the repression of the dangerous physical urges Debbie's kidnapping represents. After the failure of the second quest, Ethan and Marty return to the Jorgenson farm, where Marty and Laurie engage in traditional courtship play of the kind that leads to marriage. During this segment, Ethan evokes the question of the inheritance of property when he speaks of Aaron's herd as his rather than Debbie's. By the end of the next quest segment, that question will be foregrounded further; after finding Debbie and discovering that she now considers herself "Native," Ethan writes a will disowning her and leaving his property to Marty. He also, symbolically of course, thereby designates Marty as his successor in the narrative and in the structure of the film. Marty is indeed about to take his place as the savior of community norms.

The second search concerned the dangers of sexuality; the third on which Marty and Ethan now depart concerns the dangers of trade, but those dangers are now also related to sexuality. When they trade with the Natives, Marty accidentally buys a wife. And when they meet Scar, it is in a tent in which his several wives, including Debbie, sit. This multiplication of wives coincides with Ethan's realization that patrilineal succession is endangered and that he should will his property to Marty. Fittingly, the will scene occurs in a cave, a place of connection to physical nature that is reminiscent of the underground pigsty associated earlier in the film with the mother's sexually violated body, and foreshadows the cave out of which Debbie will be retrieved in the end.

Such an accumulation of negative meanings in so structured a film makes almost mandatory a succeeding scene in which the problems posed by those negative meanings will be resolved. In the next segment Marty and Ethan return home to find Laurie about to wed Charlie, a man who is depicted as overly effeminate. Marty fights him, re-wins Laurie, who is depicted as secretly pleased by the violence exercised on her behalf, and confirms his masculinity. It is in this segment as well that Ethan agrees to hand over his gun to Clayton. These triumphs of civil norms and institutions coincide with the scene of a wedding dance, a choreographed and highly structured event that designates roles and well-rehearsed behaviors of the kind that assure community survival. The formerly tom-boyish Laurie now wears a wedding dress that makes her a fitting counterpart to the newly masculinized Marty. The successful transformation of Marty is completed at the end of this segment when he alone proves capable of deciphering Moses Harper's riddle about the location of the Native camp.

Marty and Ethan now can change places, and Marty can succeed Ethan as the defender of the community. Marty agrees to engage in the kind of violence that has been Ethan's monopoly up to this point in the story. This transformation suggests the community's acceptance of the violence Ethan represents as necessary for its survival, while Ethan joins Clayton in a more passive two-shot in planning the rescue, a move that signals Ethan's reconciliation to the norms of the community. The reassertion of community norms and the taming of Ethan's wildness are paralleled to visual motifs which underscore the degree to which the European-Americans have risen above the wilderness landscape, that nature of physical life which has hitherto been beyond their control and has dominated them visually. After a series of images in which the men ride up hills to gain a dominant point of view on nature, Ethan and Clayton look down on the Native camp. The Natives have been characterized as unstructured wanderers who call themselves "Noyake," people who say they mean to go one way, then go the other. But now their position is clearly known, and such knowledge allows the community's structure of justice to be imposed on them. The wildness of nature is now subordinate to the normative power of civilization.

A similar elevation out of or above the natural world occurs when Ethan lifts up Debbie after the attack on the Native camp. She is taken up out of the physical world of unstructured sexual life symbolized by the cave in front of which she falls. Just prior to this moment in the film, Laurie, that emblem of the appropriate civilized, domestic female role, describes Debbie in terms that emphasize the twin dangers of promiscuity and trade: "It's too late. She's a woman grown, the leavings of a thousand bucks, sold time and again to the highest bidder, with savage bairns [children] of her own." The structure of the film requires a resolution in which Debbie is elevated out of this promiscuous world of indiscriminate natural physical sexuality and placed back in the world of norms and institutions inside the community. Now she can be properly married, and now her children, rather than belonging to anyone, will belong to one man. And that will assure that property within the community can be safely transferred from generation to generation.

The characters and the moral ideals they embody are structured in relation to one another by similitude and differentiation. Ethan and Clayton, the "Reverend" who is also head of the local Texas Rangers, are opposed to one another. Ethan initially rides up to his brother's homestead out of nature and is immediately coded as a wanderer, a lawbreaker, and a rebel against civil rules. He is contrasted to Aaron who, with his wife and children, is a homemaker and a community-builder, someone who leads a settled law-abiding existence rather than a roaming one. Clayton, in contrast to Ethan, embodies the dual principles of religion and law that impose moral rules on natural wild behavior and thereby maintain peaceful communities. Ethan is a man of the gun who seems not to have a place in a civil community. Significantly, he has no wife or romantic interest.

Ethan and Marty are also paralleled and opposed to one another. Marty is like Ethan in that he is half "wild" Indian and half "civilized" white. Like Ethan, he knows Indian lore. The initial sequences depict them in parallel visual situations. Both ride in from the wilderness toward the homestead and later sit on the porch looking back at the house while facing out toward the wilderness. Their parallel contains a significant difference, however, that is determined by their relationships to women and that shapes the outcome of the narrative: Marty is linked to Laurie and to the possibility of membership in the community through marriage and family-making. Because the film will privilege community over nature, it is Marty's values that will ultimately prevail. When Ethan expresses a wish to kill Debbie, it is Marty who stands up to him and asserts his right to save her and to restore her to the community.

Civilization and nature are also distinguished in the opposition of certain kinds of action, such as gift-giving and trading or economic exchange. Gift-giving is a symbolic gesture linked to community and to the creation of reciprocal ties between people. If gift-giving implies trust, unselfishness, and reciprocal affection, the kinds of bonds that make communities, trading implies reciprocal distrust and non-affectionate relations predicated on mutual selfish gain, the kinds of actions that characterize life outside or between communities. "At your service, for a price, always for a price," Emilio Figueroa says to Ethan. In contrast, Moses Harper, who also aids Ethan, refuses money and says he only wants a "rocking chair by the fire," an emblem of his allegiance to the community and its norms.

Ethan and Marty are connected both to gift-giving and to market exchange, but each sides with gift-giving. Ethan's gift-giving to children initially situates him as an ally of community, and his ultimate act of forgiveness toward Debbie is a gift of life to her that redeems his earlier rejection of community norms— the willingness to kill a family member. As a result, his structural place changes from dangerous outsider to community savior. Marty is more associated with gifts than Ethan, and, indeed, his attempt at market exchange proves a failure when he inadvertently trades for a wife. He can only continue on his quest by accepting gifts of a horse and gun from Laurie, and, ultimately, it is to him that Ethan makes a gift of all his property. The film thus asserts the norms of community life through each of the main characters and rejects the kinds of actions such as betrayal and theft that characterize life outside the community.

Civilization depends on the repression of certain kinds of "mad" behavior. Ethan practices some of that behavior, but in the end he is restored to the reasonableness that characterizes community norms. The more dangerous madness is associated with female sexuality. The transfer of property in a civilization is rendered impossible if the right parents of children cannot be known because women are sexually promiscuous. The most important character in this regard is Debbie. She is someone who has fallen outside the civilized structure of family civilization into the nature of promiscuous sexuality associated with the Natives. In this understanding of the film, the seemingly marginal concern with sexuality, courtship, and marriage takes on greater significance. That Ethan rides in from the wilderness at the beginning of the film suggests that he occupies a structural place in relation to the European-American community that is similar to Scar's, who rides in later to violate that community. In other words, what Scar represents outside the community, Ethan represents within the community. The violence and sexual violation that come from outside are in some respects already at work within as the human nature that must be repressed in civil communities. What Scar represents is the danger of promiscuous sexuality unrestrained by community norms and unregulated by institutions like marriage. That he also disrespects private property is of course an important related theme. Ethan is not an overtly sexual character, but he bears a sexual emblem, a sword, and he submits what it represents in sexual terms to community norms by making a gift of it to one of the children. He makes Debbie a gift of another symbol of anti-communal violence—a war medal. Such symbols play the role in communal culture of mediating and regulating violent urges and of channeling them into community-sustaining ends, and when Ethan makes gifts of them to children, he symbolically surrenders his wild urges to the community. It is interesting to note that the change in human evolution that allowed institutions such as property rights and marriage to be invented was the one that allowed us to think symbolically.

No such symbols exist outside the community because, in nature, wild physicality has not been restrained and replaced with conventions, symbols, and civil forms of interaction such as the wedding ritual. When Scar stands over Debbie, in a scene reminiscent of the one in which Ethan did the same before giving her a gift, he instead blows a phallic horn that suggests precisely the degree to which he is outside the symbolic mediations that regulate sexual desire inside communities. He has hunted and found his prey; no communal ritual like marriage is required. His wild hoot stands in contrast to the ritual-based music at Laurie's wedding that permits couples to dance in highly structured ways reminiscent of the founding structural principle of the family-based community itself.

If Scar is a projection outside the community of dangers that lie within the community, the danger particularly of potentially wild sexual urges, women's natural bodies are also coded as part of that danger. They are available to

FIGURES 16.2 & 16.3 *The Searchers*. Images of community rituals such as a wedding dance suggest order and structure and are contrasted with images of nature that depict it as unstructured.

anyone; the patriarchal requirement of a male-dominated culture that property pass on to one's own sons is endangered by the potential promiscuousness of women's bodies. Martha, Aaron's wife, is depicted as secretly longing for Ethan, but she keeps her desire in check. When Scar destroys the community, his violence also takes the form of a sexual violation of Martha. Her restraint is juxtaposed to the Natives' absence of normative restraint. It is an important part of Marty's education that Ethan prevents him from looking inside the underground shed where the rape occurred and pushes him away protectively. Maintaining Marty's distance from the dangers associated with the maternal body and with uncontrolled physical nature will be crucial as he develops into the community savior he eventually is depicted as becoming, a role that requires distance from and control over nature.

The restoration of Debbie to the family home at the end of the film is thus symbolic of a reassertion of civilized norms over wild nature. It replicates the founding of human civilization because it represents the creation of two important human institutions—property right and family. For property to be safely passed on from generation to generation, the institution of marriage was invented to protect women from predatory sexual behavior by men. With clear knowledge of parentage, property could be passed on. And with the creation of a domestic family community, norms of mutual care could be promulgated that would become the cement of civilization.

Student Assignment: *Adam's Apples* **(2005)**

How is this film about a clash between civility and pre-civil animality? Note how the pastor comes back repeatedly to the idea of rudeness. How is that linked to his larger scheme of values?

FURTHER READING

Boyd, Bryan, On the Origin of Stories: Cognition, Evolution, Fiction.

Boyd, Bryan, Joseph Carroll, and Jonathan Gottschall. *Evolution, Literature, Film*. New York: Columbia University Press, 2010.

Cosmides, Leda, and John Tooby. "The Evolutionary Foundations of Culture", in Jerome Barkow, Leda Cosmides, and John Tooby. *The Adapted Mind*. New York: Oxford University Press, 1992.

Distin, Kate. *Cultural Evolution*. New York: Cambridge University Press, 2011.

Index